The Hardball for Women Playbook

Also by Pat Heim, Ph.D., and Susan K. Golant:

Hardball for Women

Also by Pat Heim, Ph.D.:

Learning to Lead with Elwood Chapman

Also by Susan K. Golant:

How to Have a Smarter Baby with Dr. Susan Ludington-Hoe
No More Hysterectomies with Vicki Hufnagel, M.D.
Disciplining Your Preschooler and Feeling Good About It
  with Mitch Golant, Ph.D.
Kindergarten: It Isn't What It Used to Be with Mitch Golant, Ph.D.
The Joys and Challenges of Raising a Gifted Child
Getting Through to Your Kids with Mitch Golant, Ph.D.
Finding Time for Fathering with Mitch Golant, Ph.D.
Fifty Ways to Keep Your Child Safe
Kangaroo Care with Dr. Susan Ludington-Hoe
Taking Charge: Overcoming the Challenges of Long-Term Illness
  with Irene Pollin, M.S.W.

The
Hardball for
Women

Playbook

*Strategies for Winning in Business
(and in Life)*

♦♦♦

Pat Heim, Ph.D.
Susan K. Golant

Lowell House
Los Angeles
Contemporary Books
Chicago

Library of Congress Cataloging-in-Publication Data
Heim, Pat.
    The hardball for women playbook: strategies for winning in business
(and in life) / Pat Heim, Susan K. Golant.
        p. cm.
    ISBN 1-56565-086-7
    1. Women in business. 2. Career development. 3. Corporate
culture. 4. Interpersonal communication. I. Golant, Susan K.
II. Title.
HD6053.H388   1993
650.14'082—dc20   93-21102
                                                   CIP

Lowell House
2029 Century Park East, Suite 3290
Los Angeles, CA 90067

Publisher: Jack Artenstein
Vice-President/Editor-in-Chief: Janice Gallagher
Director of Publishing Services: Mary D. Aarons
Text design: Judy Doud Lewis

Manufactured in the United States of America

*To the women who encounter
the glass ceiling and who work so hard
to break through*

Contents

***

Prologue:
Playing Hardball

•••

I t has been a year since the publication of *Hardball for Women*. And what a year it has been. I have traveled across the country hundreds of times, from Los Angeles to Portland, Oregon; Portland, Maine, to Key Largo, Florida, and all points in between, bringing my message of how unacknowledged differences between the male and female cultures can undermine communication and thwart women's progress in their careers. I have spoken to employees of multinational corporations, universities, and manufacturing firms; I have consulted with government agencies, hospitals, and industries dealing in communication and mass media, scientific research, computers, and even greeting cards.

Wherever I've delivered my message, the response has been the same. Women are eager—even hungry—to learn the lessons of Hardball. Despite the enormous strides women have made during the last two decades, the corporate world is still relatively alien territory to them. The female sector of senior management has increased by only 2 percent in the last 20 years. Like it or not, the glass ceiling still does exist.

When a woman enters the male world of business, misperceptions and miscommunications abound:

- In meetings a man speaks at length, whereas a woman speaks briefly. *The man sees the woman as uncommitted to her ideas; the woman sees the man as a hog.*

- A woman takes her turn and pauses to let others speak. A man talks over and interrupts others. *The man sees the woman as having little to say; the woman sees the man as rude.*

- A woman provides background information before she recommends an idea. A man gets to the bottom line quickly. *The man perceives the woman as talkative and wasting time; the woman perceives the man as pushy and aggressive.*

- A female executive, when giving her secretary an assignment, asks about the secretary's family, notices that she recently got a haircut and compliments her on it, and slips in an appeal to get the assignment done by three. A male executive throws the documents on the secretary's desk and tells her the work must be done by three. *The man perceives his female peer as wasting time on irrelevant chatter; the woman perceives her male peer as cold and insensitive.*

Why do these misinterpretations occur? Men and women grow up in different cultures and learn dissimilar lessons about "appropriate" adult behavior. Unfortunately, they are unaware of having these divergent rules. They believe that members of the opposite sex have been trained to behave as they do.

Many of the women I met in my travels asked me for a simple manual to help them understand the cultural differences that exist between men and women. And so my coauthor Susan Golant and I conceived *The Hardball for Women Playbook*, a step-by-step guide to winning at the game of business.

Based on the program delineated in our first book, this volume presents 100 business problems, brought on by the rules of the male-dominated working world, that women encounter daily in corporate life. We've even thrown in a smattering of non-work situations to show you how these rules can apply outside the work arena. Each situation is followed by a solution based on Hardball savvy and finally, by a restatement of the rule. (In some instances the issue is not gender-based, but the rule is still important to understand.) The chapters and most of the rules are ordered as they were in *Hardball for Women*.

You may read the book from cover to cover, or you may read chapters or situations pertinent to you, as the need arises. It may help your understanding, however, to peruse the chapter introductions so that you understand the basic issues.

If you have already read *Hardball for Women*, these situations and solutions will inspire you to continue using Hardball strategies. If you have not read our first book, you may wish to read it in conjunction with this one, as it provides greater detail and explanation.

The Great Cultural Divide

If you're working with someone from Japan or Pakistan who seems to comport himself a bit strangely, you're most likely to chalk it up to a culture clash. People from other nations behave differently than we do, and we learn to be tolerant of diversity.

But because American boys and girls grow up in the same families, eat the same foods, and sit in the same classrooms, we're often unaware that each gender has been raised with divergent values and standards. As a result, we use heavily loaded language to evaluate those of the opposite gender. For instance, we may think a person of the opposite sex is being belligerent or overemotional without understanding that that individual may be behaving in a manner appropriate for his or her culture.

It is not an issue of right or wrong, good or bad. Men and women live in different cultures. Disparate cultures work fine internally; it's only when they interact that problems may arise. Gender culture is particularly difficult in this respect because it is, for the most part, invisible to us.

This book will help you understand and bridge the cultural gap that exists between men and women. It will explain the differences between the male "hierarchical" structure and the female "flat" structure and how those can impinge on a woman's career progress.

The Glass Ceiling

You may have noticed that when you finished school and started your first job, you received positive evaluations of your work in the beginning. It's only after several years have passed that you begin to get feedback on issues that are hard to understand or put your hands on. Your boss may tell you, for example, that you're "not a team player," that you're "too scattered," or that you're not "leadership material." You may have no idea what these terms actually refer to or how to correct the problem.

Or, if you are a supervisor or manager, you may find that your employees are highly committed and productive, but that the other managers at your level are the ones receiving the promotions and opportunities. This is what keeps the glass ceiling in place.

These difficulties may occur because initially you were evaluated on your technical skills; your interpersonal skills had little to do with your success. As you continue to work and climb the corporate ladder, however, your interpersonal skills come to the fore. And, because you're in a higher position, you're apt to be judged more frequently by men who unconsciously use the lens of their culture to assess your interactive style.

The Hardball for Women Playbook will give you the guidelines you'll need to break through this barrier.

Why Do I Have to Do It His Way?

As you read the situations, solutions, and rules in this handbook, you'll probably notice that for the most part they explain how men see the world and suggest ways that you can adapt.

You may find this distasteful. Indeed, the women I have encountered often wonder why they have to adjust to male mores. Again, it may help to think of the issue in cultural terms: If you went to Japan or Pakistan to work, you'd have to figure out how to adapt to those cultures in order to be successful. The same holds true in the corporate world today. Unfortunately, business is still a man's game. As a result, men are still often making those all-important judgments about who gets to join their lofty ranks.

When women do get into executive row, they can begin to change the rules. But that can only occur when they have acquired the power by playing the game using (or at least understanding) the men's rules.

How This Book Can Help

The Hardball for Women Playbook will help you learn how to read and exploit coded verbal and nonverbal messages, how to be a good team player, how to be assertive without being perceived as obnoxious, how to get your ideas heard during a meeting, how to engage in smart self-promotion, how to grow from criticism and extend praise, how to gain promotions and raises—in short, how to play Hardball the way men do.

This book will provide you with the strategies you'll need to thrive and survive in the male-dominated business place and the male-dominated world at large.

The Ground
Rules

◆◆◆

I n our culture, boys and girls live in different worlds. Males grow up and live their entire lives in hierarchies. The games little boys play, such as basketball, baseball, football, cops and robbers, cowboys and Indians, and war, are hierarchical. Sports are structured as pyramids with coaches at the top; team captains, star players, and average players in the middle; and bench warmers at the bottom. In imaginative games such as cowboys and Indians, youngsters jockey for position and advantage. Someone always wins and someone always loses.

Girls live in a "flat" social structure. They play games in which power is shared equally. There is never a captain doll player or a winner in a game of nurse. Girls who try to order others around or push ahead of their playmates are usually called bossy and have few friends.

Boys' games are goal focused. A boy would never say, "Let's get started with the game and figure out where the goal line is later." The purpose of playing is to win—to score the most points. By contrast, the main thrust of girls' play in such games as house or school lies in relating to others. There is no winning or losing. Girls pay attention to what's happening in the moment—the process of play rather than the goal.

Finally, boys play in large groups; relationships between each other are secondary to reaching the goal. Girls play one-on-one with best friends. As a result, preserving relationships is a central component in the female culture but is less important in the male culture.

The impact of these differences on the business world is profound. Men continue to perceive business as they do sports: It is a hierarchical game with goals. Not surprisingly, women see business as a web of relationships that moves forward in a continuous process. Relationships with co-workers are tools men use to get the job done. For women, such relationships are a key part of their personal lives. Because men are hierarchical, they view everyone in the organization—even peers—as either above or below them. Women tend to see co-workers, from executives to mail clerks, as being on a more equal footing. In fact, a key tenet of the female culture is the "power-dead-even rule," which means that power is always shared equally and no one is ever better than or above anyone else.

When you understand these hidden cultural differences—the ground rules of Hardball—you'll be better equipped to succeed at the game. The following situations, solutions, and rules will help you do just that.

1. The Situation:
A male co-worker is your peer but is giving you orders.

You are an account manager for a company that creates strategic plans for organizations. Your company has just landed a major client in the retail apparel business. You and your colleague Roger have both been assigned this plum account.

Things start off smoothly, but suddenly you find that Roger is critiquing your work, giving you directions, telling you that he knows the ropes in the clothing industry, and implying that you should therefore listen to him. You are surprised because the two of you are equals (actually, neither of you has a great deal of experience in this area), but he's acting like the boss. You're confused. You don't know whether to tell him to buzz off or to listen to him, since you begin to believe that perhaps the boss has instructed him to take the lead and behave in a manner that you perceive as patronizing. What should you do?

The Solution:

Despite the fact that you and your male co-worker are on absolutely equal footing, he may throw his weight around to establish his position above you in the hierarchy. Indeed, he may be testing the waters to see how far he can rise above you. Men jockey for position with their male peers, too. You may be equals in title, but to a man's eye you're either one step up or one step down. All of his communication negotiates and assesses this hierarchical structure.

Consequently, you will need to communicate indirectly to Roger that you are at the same level in the hierarchy. He might criticize your work, for example, saying, "Common sense would tell you that you don't need to provide that much numerical data in your reports."

Instead of believing him and wondering how you could be so stupid, you can respond: "I've been doing these reports for years, and no one has complained about the numbers. What leads you to conclude that in the apparel industry we need to provide a different kind of report?" You may know what you're doing, but you still don't want to lose the opportunity to learn and gain insight.

Say that, on another occasion, Roger instructs you to do the first half of a project that you've been assigned to do together. Rather than immediately following his directions, stop for a minute and consider whether you want to go along with his plan. You may wish to challenge his approach and offer alternatives. Even if you think Roger's way is best, you will still need to stop and ask, "Whoa, aren't we going to talk about this?"

Make sure that Roger doesn't get away with pushing you around. But also keep in mind that his real agenda is to test you—not to be a jerk (although that's how his behavior might look to you).

Rule: Don't allow yourself to be shoved into a one-down position with a male peer.

---

2. The Situation:
You're torn between listening to your supervisor or your heart.

You're a medical intern, and you're delivering your first baby. Although the birth went without a hitch, the actual scene is a mess! You hadn't anticipated that. You're in the process of cleaning up the delivery table when the male physician who is supervising you stops you and says, "Don't do that. That's the nurse's job."

You glance over at a still-clean nurse, who has just walked into the room, and wonder why your supervisor would have you stop in the middle of this and inconvenience the nurse by having her get messed up. Should you tell him that you'd be happy to finish it, which could irritate him, or should you turn to the nurse and ask her to do it, which would surely irritate her?

The Solution:

Medicine is a hierarchical culture, whereas in nursing, the power is shared more equally. When you try to accommodate these conflicting structures, you can become caught in between.

Bear in mind, however, that your success or failure at this point will be determined by the physician supervising you, and he comes from the hierarchical structure. He expects you to do what he says, which in this instance includes demonstrating your "physician power" to the nurse. Your professional success hinges on his evaluations, so he's the one whom you must follow at this moment, no matter what that does to your relationship with the nurse. You can grease the wheels of your alliance with her later by interacting on the personal level that women value and find so comfortable.

Rule: You work in a hierarchy; protect your position.

---

3. The Situation:
Your husband gets upset when you don't follow his advice.

You're having trouble deciding whether you should take the new job you've been offered. You approach your husband and go over the pros and cons with him. You ask, "Adam, what do you think I ought to do?"

Adam replies, "If it's such a problem for you, just stay where you are." You thank him for his input and then solicit advice from several other friends and colleagues over the next several days. Finally, you decide to accept the new position since that seems to make the most sense to you.

When Adam hears that you didn't take his advice, he throws up his hands and says, "If you were going to ignore what I said, why did you bother asking me in the first place?"

You don't understand why your husband is so upset.

The Solution:

As Adam saw the situation, you posed a problem to him, and, being the good husband he is, he solved it for you. But you weren't asking him to solve your problem; you wanted to discuss the various alternatives so that you could make the best decision for yourself.

You've run into trouble because, like most men, Adam is goal oriented. He wants to solve the problem. You, on the other hand, are process oriented. You like to talk things over with others before reaching a consensus.

In the future, when you approach Adam for input, signal to him that you are going to be talking to others before *you* make the decision. You might say, "Adam, I have this problem. I'd appreciate your take on it. I'm going to be talking to several different people about their ideas as well before I make my final decision."

If you don't prepare him, Adam will feel as if you've tricked him. You ask for his opinion and then ignore it. And as a result, he'll be less likely to lend a helping hand in the future.

The same, of course, holds true in business situations with male colleagues.

Rule: Remember that women are process oriented whereas men are goal oriented. Recognize the difference and switch to goal focus when working with a man or signal him that you're in a process mode.

---

4. The Situation:
Your boss complains that you're scattered and unfocused.

You are a human resources generalist in a department that's structured a bit differently than most. Instead of having individual managers
oversee benefits, training, compensation, and so on, your department
is organized so that managers provide all services to the employees of a
given product line.

As a former compensation manager, you've had misgivings about
this new arrangement; you have had to work in areas such as benefits
and training in which you were not an expert. Much to your amazement, however, you've come to enjoy this generalist approach, and
you have learned a great deal about human resources in the process.
Your boss has given you a lot of positive feedback about your growth
and ability to solve a wide variety of human resource problems. But six
months ago she left, and Don was hired to replace her.

You feel out of touch with Don and decide to meet with him to
bring him up to speed on your projects. During your discussion you
broach several issues: the difficulty the new director has been having
on the job, the compensation issue for the support staff, the training
program for the new E-mail system, and an idea you had to help managers solicit and implement employee input. Suddenly, Don stops you
in midsentence. Waving his hand in front of your face, he asks, "Can't
you focus on just one thing?"

You're mystified and offended. You feel as if you're producing like
crazy but clearly he doesn't see it the same way. What's going on here?

The Solution:

Men tend to live linear lives. They get out of school, go to work,
and eventually retire. For many, if not most, work is the primary focus
of their lives. This is also true of daily activities. A man might become
irritated at his wife for wanting to talk to him while he's using his
power tools. For him, it's the band saw or Mary, but not both at once.

Women's lives, on the other hand, have multiple foci. They gradu-
ate from school, go to work, pull out to have a baby, return to work
part-time and then full-time, pull out again to have a second child,
return to work, and so on. Along the way they become involved in
their children's school, community activities, and family social events.
Women live their daily lives in the same manner. They're comfortable
stirring the pot, holding the baby, opening the mail, and talking on
the phone, all at the same time.

At work, a woman engaged in several activities simultaneously may look scattered to her male boss.

It's a good bet that Don doesn't understand your ability to be effective while undertaking multiple concurrent projects. He would probably drop the ball on most of them and assumes you would, too. Moreover, he most likely can't explain his reaction because he's unsure of why he feels as he does. It would be wonderful if you could elucidate for him the male and female cultural differences, but he seems to be a rather closed person.

If you want to succeed with Don, you may have to drop most of your projects and work on only one. If that's impossible or unpalatable, continue on as you have been, but speak to him about only one project at a time. Otherwise, he will continue to see you as performing poorly.

Also, you might want to dust off your résumé. Don doesn't sound like a supportive manager who is rooting for your success.

Rule: Focus on one item at a time when working with men.

---

5. The Situation:
A female co-worker gets promoted.

Betty's promotion to assistant vice president was announced this morning. She has been your peer, but now, particularly because of her great performance on a project, she is one level above you.

In the hallway you hear a group of women talking about how "the boss has a thing for blondes," which in their opinion is obviously why Betty got promoted. Should you say anything?

The Solution:

The female culture's power-dead-even rule runs absolutely counter to the male hierarchical culture. Betty has done a good job in this male culture. Consequently, she has earned a promotion. But Betty's achievement has created disequilibrium in the usual order for her female co-workers. In their effort to reestablish a sense of normalcy, they attempt to pull her back down to her former station by disparaging her accomplishment.

Because women must support each other in their successes (if we hope to be able to get to the top of the pyramid and change the system), you should stop and enter the conversation. You can say, "I was delighted to hear about Betty's advancement. I believe she has been promoted for a variety of very good reasons." Cite a number of her recent successes and summarize by saying, "Isn't it wonderful to see that the company is promoting women?"

Then, to lighten up the situation (so that the other women don't perceive you as talking down to them, again violating the power-dead-even rule), you might laugh and add, "This place has been an old-boy club for too long, don't you think?"

Rule: Avoid sabotaging other women who receive promotions or accolades.

---

6. The Situation:
Your secretary resists your work assignments.

You notice that your male colleagues can simply throw work on Helen's desk and demand that it be done by a certain hour. She produces for them. But if you behave in exactly the same way, you rarely get the work on time, and if you do, it is shoddy.

You observe, however, that the work does get done if you say to Helen, "Well, how are you? You look great. Did you get your hair cut? I like it. How has your mom been feeling? I heard she had been sick. I'm so glad to hear she's doing better. If you could fit it in, would you mind typing this by 3 o'clock?"

Why do you have to jump through hoops with the department secretary while men don't?

The Solution:

Girls don't give directives to their playmates. Instead, they negotiate by establishing good relationships. You've got to create a good rapport with Helen if you're going to get the outcome you desire. If you don't, she will make you pay in some way. It's not fair but that's the way the female culture works. As you have correctly observed, Helen doesn't expect personal interactions from the men. Still, she works for them without complaining because she didn't grow up in the flat structure with them and thus has different expectations of them.

Rule: Create relationships with other women to get what you need.

7. The Situation:
You introduce women more informally than you do men.

You work in a major electronics firm. When executives from another company visit your plant, the vice president of operations asks you to escort them around. Your guests had prearranged meetings with managers of various departments. At the end of the day, the visitors thank you for your time and effort and seem to have enjoyed their tour.

But June Frost, one of the managers with whom they met, stops by to see you after the visitors have left. In a polite but firm way, she points out that when you introduced the guests to her male colleagues, you addressed each colleague as Mr. So-and-So, but when you introduced her, you simply used her first name. "In the future, please treat us all the same," she asks.

You don't remember doing this, but even if you did, you wonder if June isn't being overly sensitive. After all, if you did introduce her by her first name, it's because you like her more than the men and feel more comfortable with her. Is there any crime in that?

The Solution:

Because of the flat female culture of our childhood, women are likely to equalize power with women but assign power to men. They often do this unconsciously and without malice, but it can cost women dearly. As a result of your lopsided introduction, June could lose power in the eyes of her male colleagues who perceive the workplace as a hierarchy. By taking away her title (Ms., Mrs., or Miss) and last name, you inadvertently communicated that June was unequal to her male colleagues. And given how hierarchical men can be, this could be damaging. In the future, exercise caution in your introductions.

You can also explain to June your motivation in introducing her by first name only, and then tell her that you won't make that mistake again.

Rule: Don't take power away from women and hand it to men.

---

8. The Situation:
You're unsure how to introduce yourself.

You've been elected president of the medical staff of a large prestigious medical center. Yet when you attend professional meetings, you find that you introduce yourself by saying, "I'm with a facility in New York." You never mention which one or your position there because you don't want to brag. Yet you find that your ideas are dismissed out of hand. You don't want to throw your weight around. What should you do?

The Solution:

Having grown up in a culture where the power-dead-even rule requires you to play down your power, it makes perfect sense for you to avoid tooting your own horn. But, in the hierarchical culture in which you are now working, if you obscure how powerful you truly are, you will fail to have the impact you want on discussions, ideas, or meetings.

In interacting with other women, it may be appropriate to downplay your position. But if you find yourself in a male game, let the men know directly who you are and the power that you wield. When you introduce yourself, for example, explain that you're with that prestigious institution and add which important post you hold. This may feel to you like bragging, but in the male culture it's essential.

Rule: Accept reality; embrace your power.

---

9. The Situation:
A senior woman appears bitchy.

You've recently been hired into a school district that has the distinction of having a female superintendent. Since 95 percent of all the superintendents in your state are men, you were looking forward to working in an organization run by a woman.

But it doesn't take long for you to begin hearing stories about Maria. Apparently she's just like the men: She tells people what to do instead of listening to them, she's short and clipped in her communication style, and she plays politics.

You're disappointed and wonder, When a woman makes it to the top, does she have to act just like a man?

The Solution:

What kind of woman did you think would make it into the superintendent ranks? Maria couldn't possibly play by the rules of the feminine game *and* break through the glass ceiling.

Women who have reached the upper echelons have had to play many games of Hardball, which can get bloody at more senior levels. Indeed, for women to stay at the top, they must continue to play by the old-boy club rules, even if they prefer to use their more feminine strengths. They'll have to keep at it until their ranks grow and they have enough clout to change the rules.

It's unfortunate that the women in your school district don't appreciate Maria's dilemma and encourage her. She is, after all, caught between two cultures. Why not be the first to support her and point out her accomplishments to colleagues? You could help immensely by explaining to your co-workers that Maria has one foot in each world.

Moreover, you can reinforce Maria's hard-fought successes. Say to her, for example, "I really appreciate your going to bat for us to get those computers. I heard the battle was pretty hairy. I'm glad you won."

Rule: Executive women get caught between two cultures. Support them even if they appear to be power hungry, difficult, or mean—in short, bitchy.

---

10. The Situation:
You're always burned out by 5 p.m.

You find yourself exhausted at the end of the day, whereas Kenneth, your male colleague, isn't. After a series of meetings, he seems energized, but you feel like collapsing. Is this a physiological problem, or could there be some other reason?

The Solution:

Throughout the day, you are constantly adapting to a foreign culture. Before you speak, you must consider how someone who has been brought up in a hierarchical world will hear and interpret your words. You need to shape your messages so that others read your intent accurately. If not, you may repeatedly find yourself shut out of job advancement without knowing why.

To succeed at Hardball, you must remain conscious of the quality of your interactions as perceived through the lens of the male culture. This will take more energy on your part than it will for your male colleague. Eventually, however, as more women reach the top of the hierarchy and begin to incorporate the female culture into the business world, this situation will begin to change for the better. At that time interactions will be less taxing for you.

Rule: Organizations can be alien territory for women. Learn the rules of Hardball as played by the men in the workplace.

2

Competition and Conflict: The Rules of Engagement

◆◆◆

For men, competition is fun, but for women, it's painful.

Boys grow up playing competitive games. Another word for competition is conflict: me against you; us against them. Competition doesn't affect relationships; in fact, it can enhance them.

From a girl's point of view, competition damages relationships, so girls are apt to avoid conflict or look for win-win outcomes. In fact, rather than confronting a girlfriend directly about a problem, a youngster may tell others about the situation in the hope that that will "fix" it.

Because competition is difficult and alien for women, we haven't learned strategies to help us deal with it in the workplace. The following Hardball situations will help you handle competition and conflict.

1. The Situation:
You handle a conflict by avoiding a confrontation.

You are engaged in a project that must be finished immediately. Jane, your co-worker, is occupied with a proposal that's not due for two weeks. You approach her to ask for some much-needed assistance. Her response: "I can't help you now. I'm busy."

So, you slog through the work, staying late at the office and coming in early the next morning to complete it. You feel resentful toward Jane. She didn't offer to help you, even though your need was immediate and hers wasn't.

Later that day, while having lunch with some other colleagues, you mention that Jane was uncooperative when you were so swamped. You even bring it up with your boss at an afternoon meeting and with another co-worker the following morning.

Jane becomes aware that you have been talking behind her back and becomes furious. Now your small problem has become a large one. What might have been a more effective approach?

The Solution:

In their attempt to preserve relationships, women may use indirect communication, hoping that a third party will convey their grievances to the source of the resentment. This usually backfires, heightening tensions between the parties and causing small problems to grow into large ones.

When you have an issue with someone, tell him or her directly even though it may feel uncomfortable at the moment. You might have said, for instance, "Jane, I'd like to talk with you about something that happened yesterday. I needed you to help me, and I felt that you didn't care how swamped I was."

Most likely, Jane would have responded, "Well, there was a crucial memo I had to get off by the end of the day too," or "Gee, I didn't realize how important this was to you." Even if she were unable to help, your direct communication would have preserved your relationship; hidden resentments can impact it. And if she started to defend her actions, you could have simply said, "I just needed you to know how I felt. I didn't want to carry these negative feelings around inside me and have it undermine our relationship."

Rule: Use a direct approach to conflict; it will often work better in the long run.

---

2. The Situation:
A friendly co-worker attacks your ideas.

You're in a meeting, presenting a proposal over which you have been slaving for months. No sooner have you stated your position when Peter jumps in with 40 reasons why it won't work. You feel shocked and upset. You had not anticipated Peter's challenge. After all, your relationship seemed strong. You think of Peter as a buddy and are dumbfounded by his attack. Peter now seems like an enemy, and you begin wondering what you might have done to provoke this unexpected blitz.

The Solution:

For a man, encounters such as these are just part of the game. He may be trying to score points, look good for the coach (the boss), or move up in the hierarchy in relation to others (including you) at the meeting. But for a woman, attacks feel like a direct assault on the alliance.

Avoid personalizing such behaviors. If you tell yourself, "I thought we were friends. What is Peter saying about our relationship?" then you are taking his verbal assault literally and personally. Instead, realize that Peter's actions are unrelated to your relationship and do not affect it; he did not mean them in that way. He sees the encounter as a game (you're on the opposing team at the moment) and not as commentary on whether you are his buddy.

In the meeting, fight for your ideas, putting Peter's down if necessary, and realize that your counterattack won't damage the relationship if you don't let it.

Don't become paralyzed by a surprise attack. Remember, you're on the playing field and you have to run interference for your ideas, even if that means knocking Peter over!

Rule: For men, business is a game.
Don't personalize attacks.

---

3. The Situation:
A male co-worker acts as if nothing happened after a conflict.

You're still reeling from Peter's attack at the meeting. You're furious that he would turn on you, and you're sure that your relationship with him is permanently damaged. Besides, you had to defend your ideas so vehemently during his onslaught, pointing out the weaknesses of his arguments to such a degree, that you are sure you made him look bad in the boss's eyes. You never want to work with Peter again. But as you leave the meeting and silently lament the loss of colleagueship, Peter approaches you and asks, "How about lunch?"

This shocks and disorients you. In fact, you're unsure if you can be civil with this man during a meal. You even fantasize dumping his salad on his head! Should you accept his invitation?

The Solution:

In sports, it's common for boys on opposing teams to do whatever they must to destroy the opposition during the game. Yet they have no problems going out for Cokes and pizza once the game is over.

The same can be said of business meetings. For Peter, when the meeting was over, so was the game. In his view, the relationship, which had been temporarily stretched and distorted like a rubber band, now returned to its natural shape.

Should you have lunch with Peter and behave as if nothing untoward has happened? Certainly. Avoid rehashing his attack over your burgers. And be prepared. This situation will probably recur. Don't be caught off guard just because you have a good rapport with Peter. Remember, to him, business is just a game.

Rule: When the game is over, it's over. Move on.

---

4. The Situation:
You're torn between being liked and getting the job done.

You're chairing an important project for your company. As your work progresses, you realize that the people on your committee have differing ideas about how the group should proceed. Indeed, they have now divided themselves into two opposing camps. You feel torn because you realize that whatever decision you make, you're going to alienate half your committee.

You try to control the damage in advance, calling certain key committee members to talk about the pros and cons of the opposing view, in the hope they'll think the alternative has some value or they'll come up with a compromise. But eventually it becomes clear that no matter which way the decision goes, half your colleagues will be angry with you.

Besides, you have personal biases and needs. Some of the people on the side you do not favor are your good friends. Now you wish you had never accepted this responsibility; you fear losing friendships.

The Solution:

When boys play, they focus solely on winning. They don't care if Johnny is upset because he didn't get a turn at bat. Girls cringe at the thought of hurt feelings. It is natural, then, that you are moved to care about the friendship aspect of your decision.

Explain the decision process logically to your committee, walking them through it with you, asking them to look at all of the factors involved. Stay focused on what is best for the organization, not the individual. Then, make the decision that benefits the organization regardless of relationships. Your friends may lose power, position, and influence, but in the long run they're likely to see that your decision was best for the company.

If, however, you choose to make your decision based on who will like you as a result of it, you can never win. Someone will always be disgruntled with you or your choices. Keep in mind that your goal is to do what's best, not to be liked. Face facts: Having power means being responsible for decisions, and rarely will everyone agree with your decisions.

Rule: If you can't be both liked and respected, make sure you're respected.

---

5. The Situation:
You're pressured to make changes quickly.

You are hired into a department that has a lot of problems. In particular, customer complaints are high and the department is overbudget. In hiring you, Dave explained that you had to solve these problems in two months. You feel up to the challenge.

You begin to gather ideas and input from your employees about the causes of the problems. You have a sense of what should be done, but you don't want to "boss" anyone around, especially since you're new, so you make no changes, waiting for the employees to come to a consensus and agree with your ideas.

After the first month, Dave calls you into his office and says, "I hired you to take care of these problems, but since you started here, nothing has changed. You have one more month or you'll need to look for another job."

What should you do?

The Solution:

Boys are used to taking directions from the coach. Girls, on the other hand, tend to collaborate on ideas and decision making. In fact, collaboration is how decisions are made when power is shared equally.

Unfortunately, being bossy is just what you need to do when placed in a time-bound position of responsibility. Your employees may dislike you in the short run (see Situation #4), but it is unrealistic for you to expect that all of them will like you anyway.

It would help if you told your department in advance that changes must be made over the next month. You can say, "I appreciate your input. It has helped me understand how these problems can be solved." Then, take charge and begin making and implementing the required changes. Collaboration and consensus would be nice if you had the luxury of time, but you don't.

Rule: It's nice if you can collaborate in making decisions, but at times you'll just have to give the order.

---

6. The Situation:
You have a problem with a co-worker.

Certain reports are supposed to be delivered to your department by noon daily so that your department can consolidate them by the end of the day. Carol, the manager of the accounts payable department, is chronically late in getting her reports to you.

This irritates and frustrates you, since Carol's delay diminishes your department's productivity. Many of you can't move forward on your work until you have the accounts payable reports in hand.

Finally, one day you've had enough and you storm over to Carol's office and say, "I can't believe how self-centered you are! You don't care about my department, you only care about yours. Besides, your employees are lazy and inconsiderate. Why can't you get your reports in to me on time?"

The conversation quickly escalates into an argument. Carol feels forced to defend herself and her employees and to attack you and yours. You reach no solution.

What could you have done differently?

The Solution:

Whenever an individual feels that she has been attacked personally, she naturally becomes defensive. If, however, you approach her with the issue framed as a mutual problem rather than a direct and personal attack, you are more likely to resolve the conflict satisfactorily. In addition, if you speak from how you're experiencing the problem— making "I" statements about your reality, as in "I feel frustrated"— you're more likely to be heard than when you tell your co-worker what she is like, making "you" statements.

It is more effective for you to describe the situation as you are experiencing it. You could say, for example, "Carol, I'm not sure if you know this, but we depend on getting those reports by noon each day. This is important to us because it takes at least five hours to compile the information. The lateness frustrates my employees because they have to work overtime, and it's a problem for me because that overtime comes out of my budget. I'd like to talk to you about some ways of working this problem out so that we're both able to do our jobs."

Rule: Attack the problem, not the person.

7. The Situation:
Your co-worker has a problem with you.

You work in systems quality for a large drug company. You and your colleague Jennifer are responsible for implementing a corporatewide information system that would help determine the most cost-effective methods to manufacture quality products.

This project has tremendous implications for your organization. It has the potential to cut costs dramatically while still allowing the company to be the top-quality producer, thereby dominating the market.

You and Jennifer had gotten along well until you were both put on this project. For reasons that you can't quite ascertain, your relationship has soured, and the two of you rarely speak to each other. As a result, the project is not moving ahead as it should, and the creative ideas and solutions you used to formulate together seem to have dried up.

You call a meeting with Jennifer. Your agenda is to air this problem so the project can move ahead. You'd also like to start having some fun at work. And so you ask Jennifer, "What's wrong? We don't seem to talk to each other anymore."

Initially, she's vague, but finally she says, "I resent the fact that you don't support me."

You're about to assure her that you do, but you can already anticipate her response: "No, you don't." This yes-I-do, no-you-don't exchange will go nowhere fast. You wonder what alternatives you have.

The Solution:

To resolve conflicts effectively, talk only about behaviors, *never* evaluations of behaviors. For example, to tell someone "You are lazy" is an evaluation. But to say "You didn't get the report to me when we agreed" is a description of behavior. To tell someone "You have a bad attitude" is an evaluation. (*Never* use this expression; it's sure to backfire.) Instead, describe the behavior that led you to conclude she has a bad attitude. You could say, for example, "When you slam your door and drawers, I'm pretty sure something is wrong."

If you don't describe behavior and simply give feedback on laziness or attitude instead, the other person won't have a clue what to change. People become more defensive when someone evaluates their behavior, but far less so when someone describes it.

It would have been ideal for Jennifer to describe which behavior of yours was a problem for her. Instead, she gave you an evaluation: lack of support. You need to ask with curiosity and without becoming defensive, "I'm sorry I seem unsupportive to you. I didn't mean to be. What have I done that would cause you to see me that way?"

In that case, Jennifer might reply, "When I bring up ideas in the meetings you never say anything."

That would explain it all. You would answer excitedly, "Jennifer, I think we're a great team. You're the idea person and I'm the implementer. In meetings you are so creative and think up one idea after another. I'm quiet because I'm trying to figure out how to put your great ideas into action."

What could have been an argument over "support" has been avoided because you and Jennifer have described your behaviors.

Rule: During a conflict, describe rather than evaluate the other's behavior; in turn, if you receive evaluative feedback, ask for a description.

---

8. The Situation:
A co-worker uses diversionary tactics.

You call an employee in for a counseling session because he consistently comes to work late. You start to discuss Fred's tardiness when he goes on the offense, saying, "You know, you said when you hired me that after a couple of months I'd be working directly with clients. Well, I've been here six months and I still haven't met any clients. If you were a better manager, the morale in this department wouldn't be in the pits. And I'm not the only one who thinks so. People in other departments talk about how you manage. You don't know anything about how to deal with employees."

You feel confused and hurt by Fred's attack. Secretly, you have always questioned the quality of your management and now you wonder which of your colleagues has been complaining about you. Having been completely distracted from the initial issue you've raised, you don't know what to say next, but you're inclined to defend your good name.

The Solution:

It's easy to be thrown off course when your opponent unexpectedly goes on the offensive. Just bear in mind that when men have a sense that they're in a vulnerable, defensive position, they may switch tactics and suddenly take the offensive. If a woman falls into this trap and starts defending herself, *she* is now in the vulnerable position and is more likely to lose this battle of wills. This strategy works particularly well on women because they're more apt to find fault with themselves.

Don't lose sight of the goal, which in this instance is dealing with Fred's tardiness. Sidestep his attack by saying, "We're not here to talk about my management style. This discussion is about the fact that you have been late three times this week."

Fred, in fact, may be a "kitchen sink" fighter—that is, he throws everything at you, including the kitchen sink. If so, he is likely to continue hurling every complaint he can think of. Your task is to redirect the conversation and stay on the offensive. Repeat in the old broken-record technique, "We're not here to talk about me. We're here to talk about the fact that you've been late three times this week." With persistence, you'll eventually be able to control the conversation. (Also see situation #4 in this chapter regarding being respected versus being liked, and chapter 8 on self-talk.)

Rule: Stick to the issue at hand.

9. The Situation:
You get defensive when a co-worker attacks.

You and your colleague Josh rarely see eye to eye. That wouldn't bother you so much, but it seems you always end up on the losing side of your argumentative discussions, slinking away to lick your wounds.

Josh storms into your office shouting, "Why did you recommend to the regional VP that we provide him with weekly instead of monthly numbers? That's the most stupid-ass idea I've ever heard. Where the hell was your head, or were you just brown-nosing?"

You're angry and offended by Josh's language, but you're also tongue-tied. You start to defend your suggestions by saying, "Well, I thought it would help with the inventory problem that Charles has been complaining about," but you know you sound like a wimp, so you change your tactics. "I don't like you using that kind of language with me," you sputter. Now you sound like an ancient schoolmarm. Is there any hope?

The Solution:

During a game, boys learn to go on the offensive so that they don't find themselves on the defensive. Men often take the offensive right away, especially if they're unsure about their position. Girls don't learn this tactic as they grow up. Consequently, when women are put on the defensive they take this as an attack that can damage or even destroy relationships.

Men will often swear as a way to express power in order to get one up in the hierarchy. Women, who have long been admonished against swearing (it's not "ladylike"), can be thrown off or offended by it.

Recognize Josh's strategy for what it is, and respond to him by going on the offensive yourself. You could say, "You know darn well that weekly reports are the best way to take care of the inventory problem." Don't respond to the swearing, even if it offends you. If Josh knows that these words push your buttons, he'll just keep on using them.

**Rule: If you find yourself on the defensive,
switch to the offensive.**

---

10. The Situation:
You're the target of a game of attack.

You're giving a presentation to a group of executives. Five minutes into your talk, several of them start to attack you. Their comments range from "Well, little lady, if you hadn't just gotten out of business school, you'd probably understand reality a lot better," to "We've been successful so far. We must be doing something right around here."

Although you feel overwhelmed by the sheer number of people challenging you, some of the attacks are not quite so vicious. Michael, for example, says, "That might be a good idea to implement at another time."

You have no idea how to cope with so many challenges. Should you answer them one at a time or all at once? Should you address specific issues? Should you look to Michael for support?

The Solution:

During a game of attack, most of the men will be following the leader. Unfortunately, a woman unaware of this strategy may try to resolve the conflict by appealing to the man who seems the most reasonable and the least threatening, but who probably is not the instigator.

You need to figure out who the leader is. Watch the group. The other men may look at him (either for cues or nods of approval) or pick up on his train of thought. Sometimes you can identify him by his physical stance; he will have pulled himself up and gotten bigger. He may be the loudest of your critics or he may be the top executive in the room, although this is not always true.

To defend yourself in a game of attack, ignore everyone else and deal with the leader. Whatever your outcome with him, it will mirror your outcome with everyone else.

What do you say to him? First, be sure not to take the attack personally. Get back into the logic of your position; focus on why you thought it was a good idea in the first place. Restate the problem, saying, "We're losing market share at the rate of 2 percent a quarter. We can't afford to continue in this way. The new strategy I'm proposing will stem this hemorrhage." Keep going back to your logic and dominating the meeting with the discussion of your ideas. (See chapter 6, situation #3 for more on how to hold the floor in a meeting.)

**Rule: If you're the target of a game of attack,
take out the leader first.**

3

Do What the
Coach Says

◆◆◆

On a team, the coach is always on top. He determines how much you get to play and gives advice in the form of criticism and praise. Coaches expect you to do what you're told without question. In fact, challenging the coach or running your own play elicits the punishment of a hundred push-ups or exclusion from an important game. Coaches will assert their authority in a variety of ways and expect players to abide by it.

The concept of coaching doesn't factor into a flat structure. In the female culture, everyone negotiates different opinions, and the best option is chosen based on what's fair for all. Questioning is the means by which girls flesh out and resolve potential opportunities and problems. They often reach a decision for action by collaboration and consensus. There's no coach in playing dolls or house.

Because women are unfamiliar with the hierarchical structure, they benefit from being coached by others who know the playing field and its obstacles well. The rules in this chapter will help you understand how to play along.

1. The Situation:
Your boss gets irritated when you ask questions.

You are a vice president at a large corporation. Whenever the CEO, an ex-marine, assigns you a project, you want to understand the whys and wherefores so you can produce the outcome he wants. But when you launch into these questions, he angrily cuts you off and barks, "Look, I gave you the assignment. Just do it."

The Solution:

The boss sees himself as the coach. In his mind he has given the ball to you, the player, and told you to run with it. But much to his amazement, you want to talk about the play, which sounds to him as if you are questioning his authority, even though you are not. He misses the real intent, which is your need to gain as complete an understanding as possible of this assignment in order to do a good job.

With this kind of boss, you would be wise to take the assignment, no questions asked, and start working on it. If you're really stumped, solicit input from co-workers and colleagues who have experience in this area. Once you have actually produced something, you can return to the boss for some "coaching."

Rule: Just do what you're told.

2. The Situation:
Your company makes unreasonable requests of you, including your giving up weekends to work.

You work for a large accounting firm and are hoping to make part-ner someday. You find, however, that this company has the peculiar habit of scheduling important meetings at which your presence is demanded on the opposite coast at a moment's notice. Most often, the meetings are early Monday morning, meaning you must sacrifice your Sunday as well. You're mystified as to why your superiors aren't more thoughtful. After all, with a bit more preplanning and scheduling, you wouldn't have to lose a Sunday. The company prides itself on its effi-ciency and you wonder why they can't get their act together when arranging these meetings.

The Solution:

These last-minute meetings are intentionally scheduled to require you to give up your Sunday, thus inconveniencing you personally. The real agenda behind them is to determine whether you are loyal to the company. Which would you put first: the company or your personal needs? Your superiors can't measure your loyalty unless they make their demands significant. At times these demands may even be excessive.

If you truly want to make partner in this company, you will have to put up with many years of unnecessary and illogical demands on your personal life. Indeed, if you sincerely want to succeed in this organiza-tion, you must bite the bullet and happily appear on Monday morn-ings on the opposite coast to prove what a committed team member you are. If you don't, your rising status may be jeopardized. You may get permanently parked in your current job because the powers-that-be will perceive that you're not a team player.

Rule: Bizarre, illogical requests may be loyalty tests. As long as they're not illegal or immoral, accede to them.

---

3. The Situation:
You don't type.

You're interviewing for a position as director of marketing. In the midst of your discussion, John, one of your potential peers, walks in with a report for the boss. Larry, your anticipated new boss, takes the sheaf of papers, glances at it, and chuckles, saying, "John, I can always tell when you've typed your reports yourself."

After John leaves, Larry turns back to you, and you remark, "I never type my own reports."

The interview ends abruptly, and you are mystified when you're not selected for this position for which you're so well qualified.

The Solution:

Coaches want to believe that players will do anything the coach requests. If you demur, no matter how insignificant or unlikely it is that this request may come up in the future, the boss will interpret your response as that of a less-than-devoted team member.

Even if you absolutely refuse to perform certain work-related tasks, there is no need for you to advertise it. In fact, you're wiser to simply stay mum on these issues. If, however, your boss asks you to carry out such a task, you will need to find a way to maneuver around the assignment without confronting him. You may, for example, locate another co-worker or even hire someone to handle it for you.

A caveat here: If the boss asks you to engage in illegal or immoral activity, you probably would not want this job anyway. Those are the only situations in which you may feel safe saying, "Sorry, Larry. I just won't do that."

Rule: Never say never.

---

4. The Situation:
Your boss resists your great idea.

You're an assistant professor of French on the department's curriculum committee. The group has been restructuring the core curriculum. You would like to add several contemporary authors to the modern literature reading list, but every time you bring up your ideas, Claude, the department head, deflects them. A specialist in the Middle Ages, he frowns on the avant garde.

It's hard for you to accept Claude's refusal because you're sure that once he sees how exciting this new material is and how involved the students will become, he will understand what a great contribution to the department it actually is. And so you begin teaching this new literature without his approval. At the end of the first 10 weeks of the semester, you show him your students' excellent essays. Much to your surprise, he responds gruffly and abruptly excuses himself to attend a meeting.

As time passes, you find that Claude talks to you less and excludes you from important meetings that you had attended before. Where have you erred?

The Solution:

Coaches know that they won't always come up with the solution to a problem, but they still expect their players to do what they're told—period. Consequently, a boss is likely to see an employee who goes against his authority and decisions as a loose cannon. It doesn't matter how well the situation turns out. The bigger issue for him is that you don't understand your position in the hierarchy. Inadvertently, you have challenged his power, and now he must demonstrate that he is in charge. He does this by ignoring and excluding you.

If Claude nixes your proposal, recognize that you can't implement it yourself. You will need his support and, in some ways, his participation. The best strategy is to convince him that this is such a good idea that he should take it on as his own. For example, you might say, "I was at a meeting at which other faculty were talking about what a great job you've been doing upgrading the curriculum. It seems as if you're really getting a name for innovation at the university. What do you think about adding a couple of new authors to the reading list?" You may also want to enlist some of your peers to campaign for the new curriculum.

If Claude responds negatively, bide your time and wait for another opportunity down the road. On the other hand, if he says, "I'd like to, but the students are already complaining that they've got too much reading," you might answer, "I've got some essays and short stories we might add without creating too much of a burden."

**Rule: Coaches want you to behave like a follower;
save your own good ideas for later.**

---

5. The Situation:
Your boss takes credit for your work.

Several months ago, Joanne, your boss, had asked you to prepare end-of-the-month summaries of the department's activities. You have been writing these since and believe you have been doing a stellar job, but you have not gotten much in the way of comment from Joanne. A couple of days ago, however, you were at a meeting at which Todd, Joanne's boss, was present. He began to compliment Joanne (who wasn't even there) for her monthly summaries. He then passed one around so that everybody could see why he was so pleased.

Much to your amazement and chagrin, it was your summary that was circulating around the table. Your name had simply been removed and Joanne's put in its place. You were too shocked to speak up during the meeting. In fact, you're not even sure that you should have. But now you wonder if you should mention this incident to Joanne.

The Solution:

It can be very aggravating to find that your work has been passed off as someone else's, even if it's your boss's. But those who perceive the work world as hierarchical may believe that your work is their work, since they're supervising you. In this context, they don't see such an act as purloining your contributions.

It's important to note that good bosses will always give their employees credit because they understand that this is motivating to the employee and will likely encourage peak performance the next time. But you won't always have a good boss.

If you go against Joanne, saying, "You used my material without giving me credit," she's going to wonder if she can still count on your support and loyalty.

Instead, you might let her know that *you* know she has used your material, but you need to do so in a way that she doesn't lose face. Mention to her that Todd praised the monthly report at the meeting: "He even passed around a copy so that everyone could see the work. I was pleased to find that it was the report I had drawn up." Then, you might add, "It would be great if you somehow informed Todd about my contributions to the monthly report." This could increase your visibility and Todd's (or other superiors') appreciation of your abilities, which may open doors for you in the future.

**Rule: Allow your boss to take credit for your work.
As distasteful as it may seem, it may pay off in the long run.**

---

6. The Situation:
You get passed over for opportunities.

You're a speaker for a national management training firm. You're proud of the fact that of the 40 other speakers in this company, you are consistently ranked as one of the top two speakers on participant evaluations. So you're puzzled as to why the men always get the perk of making extra money by giving in-house programs and designing new seminars.

The Solution:

The male culture is too different for you to attempt to navigate on your own; it's hard to learn the rules of Hardball by just observing the game in play. It's important to have a mentor; at least two are preferable in case one falls out of favor or gets fired. Your mentor will take you into the culture and explain how it all works: how extra assignments are made, who has power and who doesn't, who you need to get on your side, and who to watch out for.

This has been borne out scientifically. In a recent study of 76 successful women executives, 100 percent had mentors (both male and female), and most of them even had more than one. By contrast, only 34 percent of the successful male executives in the study had mentors.

Moreover, you need someone you can consult about how to handle difficult situations. You can't just depend on the feedback you get from your boss to make the male culture clear to you. Also, in meetings a mentor will protect you from attack and underline your contributions.

Unless your company has a mentorship program in operation, you simply can't ask someone to be your mentor. Typically, mentorships develop in much the same way friendships do. You might have an opportunity to work together, find that you enjoy each other, and begin asking some questions. Your senior may take pride in offering insight into the organization.

You need not formalize the relationship by asking "Would you be my mentor now?" any more than you would pose that question to a new friend. You will take coaching from your mentor just as you would from your boss.

You might drop by to ask your mentor, "Please explain to me how these special assignments are handed out. Who should I talk to? What should I do? Is there some informal system I should be aware of?" Your mentor will help you understand how the system works so that you, too, can plan new programs and take on more power.

Rule: You need a mentor to help you figure out a game plan for advancing your career.

4

How to Be a Team Player

◆◆◆

Men and women define being a team player in different ways. Men see team membership as knowing one's position and playing it well without question even if it's painful. They are committed to their team, demonstrating their loyalty by working with others they dislike, speaking a common language, following orders they believe are inappropriate, and even dressing in the team uniform.

Women believe that being a good team player means listening to one another, working together collaboratively, and helping anyone they can in any way they can. (This harkens back to the flat structure.) They see themselves as independent individuals within an organization. Their connection to the group comes through relationships with friends. If a woman believes a decision is inappropriate, she's more likely to take a personal stand against it. She's also reluctant to work with people she dislikes; it seems two-faced.

Nevertheless, despite their strong seasonal team affiliations, in playing sports boys often switch from one team to another in successive seasons. Their relationship with former team members can change as easily as taking off one jersey and putting on another. They're friendly competitors, but they're still competitors.

Girls, on the other hand, make long-lasting commitments to friends and are likely to remain loyal through thick and thin. To them, it would be deceitful to compete with those they consider friends. The situations in this chapter will teach you how to be a team player the Hardball way.

1. The Situation:
You believe you don't need anyone's help because nobody can do a job as well as you. On the other hand, you believe others should be able to do their own work.

As a meeting planner, you're tops; you do the work assigned you flawlessly. Your boss has told you how much he appreciates your output, but he has also criticized your unwillingness to pitch in and help others. For example, you won't answer your colleagues' phones or step in to deal with their clients in a pinch. You believe these tasks are outside your responsibility. In fact, you're critical of your colleagues since they seem unable to handle their workload on their own. On the other hand, sometimes your colleagues sabotage you by withholding helpful information or failing to come to your defense when you're unfairly attacked.

You're unclear about your role vis-à-vis your co-workers.

The Solution:

You may see yourself as an independent agent within an organization rather than as a member of a larger team. Even though you may be a top performer, however, you still need a team to allow you to maintain your level of excellence. Without one, you may miss the subtle support you require. In fact, you may find that others undermine your efforts. Your team should be broad and deep, consisting of more than just your friends and "nice" people.

Team building occurs when you help others and share information even if you don't have to. In return, your co-workers will do the same for you when you need them. While you may be a stellar employee now, it may be hard to maintain that position if others are resentful and try to pull you down. Look for opportunities to offer assistance. You'll be creating a team so that you'll have support when you need it.

Rule: Create a team in order to win.

---

2. The Situation:
A buddy turns on you.

You are an engineer working in research and development. Tom is your peer but you also have a close friendship. Both of you just got a new boss. You learn that when Tom met with Mr. Simmons, Tom was critical of your work. You feel hurt and betrayed and believe Tom is doing this just so that he gets a lead position with Mr. Simmons. What should you do?

The Solution:

Recognize that the relationship you've had with Tom is not the same as the one he has had with you. Indeed, he may be less dedicated to the relationship than you are. If it's advantageous for him to switch teams at this moment and see you as the competition, he may do so. He'll perceive this as a smart strategic move, not a violation of an undying relationship. Realize that this is common and don't take it personally. Tom is effectively playing the game of business as he understands it, and you may have to play by the same rules from time to time, trying to get in good with Mr. Simmons when you can.

Rule: Recognize that men may be friendly but won't necessarily be loyal to you, even if they're your buddies. Root for your own team.

---

3. The Situation:
You have to choose between friendships and a promotion.

You are a staff social worker and you enjoy your job a great deal. Most important, you love your co-workers, a supportive group of women who are fun to be with. You're almost like a family.

Now you get good news and bad news: You've been offered a promotion to be your co-workers' supervisor. You're concerned that if you take the promotion, it will hurt your friendships with your buddies. After all, you'll be giving them assignments and supervising their work. You've noticed that when other staff social workers have been promoted they are no longer invited to lunch or parties with the gang. On the other hand, you would like to have opportunities to grow in this hospital. You feel torn, but right now you're leaning toward declining the position. What should you do?

The Solution:

You're right in assessing that a promotion will probably change your relationship with your co-workers. You can certainly continue to be friendly with them if you are the supervisor (having lunch together from time to time, joking around at work, or talking about family activities).

But maintaining close friendships (sharing intimate details of your lives) will make it difficult if not impossible for you to manage well, for two reasons. First, it will be hard to give negative feedback. Second, people have expectations of a friend that they don't have of a boss. For example, some of your friends will expect you to make exceptions for them that you wouldn't make for other employees. It can become a mess!

Be clear about your choices. Your options are deep friendships but professional stagnation, or professional growth but the loss of some of those close contacts. There's no correct choice here—you'll have to decide what feels right to you. If you do choose to take the promotion, friendliness rather than friendship is the appropriate relationship.

Rule: You can't have it both ways in business: Choose whether friendship or friendliness is the appropriate relationship.

---

4. The Situation:
You have to work with someone you dislike.

You're responsible for sales and marketing in a midsize publishing house. The degree to which you and your department can perform your jobs well is based on what your computer system can do for you. To date, you've had a second-rate system. You feel as if you're always fighting it.

Marge was hired this past year as the director of information systems. You've heard that she can make a computer sing, but she's arrogant, self-centered, and talks down to people. You're reluctant to make contact with her, let alone ask her for help. What should you do?

The Solution:

For men, close personal relationships are absent from the team equation. Boys want the meanest, toughest, roughest kid on the block to play on their team because that will help them win the game. On the other hand, because intimate relationships are so central in the female culture, girls won't play with people they dislike.

This cultural disparity puts you in a double bind. You can be nice to Marge and get the computer system you need (which may feel to you as if you're being manipulative and phony), or you can avoid her and continue struggling with your current set-up.

You don't have to marry Marge; you just need her to fix your computer. Realize that being socially appropriate with her is not necessarily being two-faced. By enlisting her aid, you'll be doing what you can to meet your tracking needs as fast as possible. That, and not Marge's noxious personality, should be your focus.

Rule: Because you need strong players on your team, be prepared to play with people you don't necessarily like.

---

5. The Situation:
You don't want to attend boring meetings.

Your company has ordered a whole new computer system. Management has invited several employees, including you, to participate in providing the computer company with input to customize the software.

You have attended the first couple of meetings and found them extraordinarily boring. The outside people speak in foreign tongues, and you believe these discussions are a colossal waste of your time. Should you continue attending these sessions?

The Solution:

Information is power. You potentially have the opportunity to get power from three sources in these meetings: You can help shape how information systems in your company work in the future; you will be one of the few employees who understand how this system functions and what it can do; and you can be sure that the new system allows your area to do a top-notch job in the future.

Moreover, attending these meetings is important strategically. Your superiors will see you as a concerned member of the team, willing to do what it takes to make sure the company wins.

This is another occasion in which you'll have to bite the bullet. Continue going to these meetings despite your misgivings. But use your time wisely. Get educated. Demand that the experts explain what they're talking about. For example, don't simply assume that you must try to understand their language. Put the onus on the computer techies to adapt to *you*; ask them what terms mean, and if you still don't understand, request that they approach it from a new angle. After all, they are in your service.

On the other hand, if your boss is running the meeting, you might want to temper your questions. Frame them so that it is evident you're interested and eager to get the system up and running for the benefit of your team.

Rule: Attend important meetings
even if they are boring.

---

6. The Situation:
You want to be fair but others resist your suggestions.

You're in a meeting at which the firing of Anna is being discussed. Bill says that he has talked to the outplacement firm. They recommend that Anna be called into her boss's office and told that she is being terminated (he should not spend more than five minutes doing this). Then, the security guard should escort her to her desk and stand by while she cleans it out. Finally, the guard should walk her out of the building.

You feel that this is a humiliating, unfair way to treat an employee, even if she's being fired for marginal performance. You voice your concerns about fairness but the rest of your team ignores your concerns. What can you do?

The Solution:

Men are geared to winning, and women are geared to doing what is fair for all. The men in this meeting are looking at how to protect the company and, as a result, when you continuously bring up fairness it seems an irrelevant, bleeding-heart issue to them. That's why they're ignoring your input.

Don't give up your concern about fairness to Anna, but reframe your message. Put your goal (which is to conduct this situation as painlessly and respectfully as possible) in the context of the team goals: helping the company to win. For example, you could say, "Have you thought about the backlash we'll provoke from other employees seeing us treat one of their co-workers in this way? The rumor mill will be in full tilt and productivity will inevitably go down. This method of terminating Anna will cost us more than it's worth in terms of security."

Rule: Don't expect others to be fair. Reframe your concerns in terms of win/lose for your team.

---

7. The Situation:
You suspect that someone is trying to cheat you.

You're the buyer of surgical equipment for a large health care organization. You have been seeking a particular piece of equipment, and you've decided to switch suppliers because the competition has come out with a refinement on the product that the physicians in your organization seem to favor. Hal, your rep from the surgical equipment company, dismisses this new product in the course of your meeting. He says, "My company has done a study on it and has found that it increases the risk of infection in surgical patients."

You're almost convinced, but you wonder if there's some Hardball going on here.

The Solution:

In sports, fouling, clipping, and face-masking are all illegal but "necessary." You can cheat as long as you don't get caught at it or it doesn't cost the team the game. For many men, "being strategic" or "expanding the parameters" is often how the game of business is played.

Women have a strong sense of acceptable and unacceptable behavior. They're unlikely to step over the line if it's against the rules. In fact, they may even be somewhat gullible, expecting others with whom they must deal to stick to the straight and narrow. Thus, they may not even suspect that cheating occurs all the time.

Hal may have simply made up this "study" to enhance sales so that his team can win. When you hear questionable or unlikely statements, you must require hard evidence to back them up. You may feel as if you're impugning Hal's integrity, which might affect your relationship, but keep in mind that he's playing by a different set of rules. Indeed, if he were speaking the truth, he would be only too glad to share the research with you. Get the real facts to make the best decision for your company.

**Rule: Don't be gullible: Cheating is part of the game.
If you're on the receiving end of a scam,
call the dissembler's bluff.**

---

8. The Situation:
Your ideas are ignored at a meeting.

Your community is plagued by low-flying small aircraft that land and take off from a local airport. You and several other indignant neighbors have gotten together to take action. You're able to get the issue of noise pollution placed on the airport board's agenda. You have some ideas about creating a noise abatement program.

During the meeting, you find that whenever you speak, it feels as if your words simply evaporate into thin air. None of the board members, all male, responds to your ideas; instead, they all seem to be taking a different course. It feels to you as if the plane has taken off without you. What's going on here?

The Solution:

Men resist being influenced, especially in public. To avoid the embarrassing situation of having to change their position in front of others, thereby appearing weak, men get their ducks lined up *before* a meeting.

Prior to the official meeting, members of the board have most likely already discussed how they're going to respond to your complaints, and the decision has already been made regarding what is (or isn't) going to be done during informal one-on-one discussions—perhaps on the golf course or around the water cooler. The problem is, you don't know that, and you continuously bring up your ideas in vain.

Recognize that the meeting happens *before* the meeting. Discuss your great ideas with key members of the board well in advance of the formal meeting and get their buy-in. That's when you'll have your greatest shot at influencing the ultimate outcome.

After the meeting, be sure to contact board members to ask them how they felt it went. Strategize with them on the next steps that must be taken.

Rule: Sell your ideas before and after
the scheduled meeting.

---

9. The Situation:
You don't speak top management's lingo.

The executive team is throwing around some new language. They talk about TQM, CQI, SPA, and Self-Directed Teams. You're unsure what this new alphabet soup is about and wonder why these people can't speak just plain English. You resist learning the new language, thinking that it's a passing fad.

The Solution:

Teams often develop their own language. This lingo clearly delineates who's on the inside and who's not. Whether this is a passing fad is irrelevant. You need to be able to speak the language of the powerful team, who in this case are the executives of your company. If you can't, it's easy for them to dismiss you as being uncommitted or an outsider. Take the opportunity whenever possible to read up on TQM (total quality management), CQI (continuous quality improvement), SPA (statistical process analysis), and Self-Directed Teams so that you can connect. Furthermore, share what you know with the team whenever the opportunity arises.

**Rule: Learn to speak the language
of the powerful team.**

---

10. The Situation:
You want to get your ideas across.

You're a free-lance management development consultant. You have contracted to do team building with the middle managers of a company you work with. They complain that senior management doesn't value, listen to, or appreciate them. You feel it is important to present this information to senior management, but you're uncertain how to do it so that they will hear and act on it. You fear that relationship issues such as "being valued" will seem irrelevant to senior management and, worse, will make the middle managers appear weak or emotional. How do you proceed?

The Solution:

Teams value certain goals. In fact, they are constantly scanning the horizon for opportunities to further those goals. Frame your interactions in a way that is consistent with the goals of your team, or in this case senior management.

If you bring up to this group of male executives middle management's complaints about being appreciated, feeling listened to, and being personally valued, the men may see these issues as too emotionally laden and unrelated to their business goals. Consequently, it is unlikely that they will act on these grievances.

On the other hand, you know that the senior management team values productivity and innovation. Convey the feedback in a way that helps them understand that they are losing valuable opportunities for increased productivity and creative ideas. You might say, for example, "The middle management team indicated that they would like to contribute more to help you solve productivity problems. They also talked about some creative ideas that have not yet been tapped. How can we use middle management as a resource?"

Rule: Sell to the team's goal.

---

11. The Situation:
An executive comments on your clothes.

You're a regional coordinator for a large personal care products company. You work in the northeast and are summoned to the home office in Kansas City for a national meeting.

You buy a stunning chartreuse designer suit just for this important occasion. At the meeting, one of the senior executives comments, "That's quite an outfit. I've never seen that color around here before."

What does he mean by that, and how should you respond?

The Solution:

We are unaware that men and women have significantly different yet subtle ways of looking at clothing. Men see clothing as the team uniform, women perceive it as an expression of self.

Most organizations have strong but unwritten rules about "appropriate" attire. Just because a dress code is omitted from the employee manual, or just because no one has said anything specific about such a code to you, doesn't mean that it does not exist. Indeed, most organizations have unwritten rules. If you violate them, you can find yourself on the outside.

This executive is sending you an indirect message that you have violated the team uniform. Observe what other executives are wearing, particularly while you have the advantage of being at the home office. If you notice that most of the men are wearing gray and navy blue suits and that the women are clad in dark, more conservative colors and suits, the message is clear that to be on this team, you'll need to dress conservatively.

Rule: Recognize your team uniform and wear it.

5

How to Be a Leader

•••

There is no single appropriate leadership style. According to management experts Paul Hersey and Ken Blanchard, four styles predominate:

 • *Directing*: The manager calls all the shots and the employee follows.
 • *Coaching*: The manager involves the employee in evaluating problems and alternative solutions but is the ultimate decision maker.
 • *Supporting*: The manager discusses problems and solutions, but the employee takes the lead in implementing ideas.
 • *Delegating*: The employee solves the problems and makes the decisions.

Effective leaders are able to choose a style based on the competence (technical ability) and commitment (capacity to carry out the task appropriately without supervision) of the employee. The more competent and committed she is, the less directive the manager needs to be.

Our female culture complicates these issues. Women often gravitate to the more collaborative approaches to leadership (coaching and supporting) because they're accustomed to sharing power with others. This is not a problem as long as the employee is ready for and needs involvement. Collaboration is inappropriate, however, if the employee is not ready (she doesn't know what she's doing or won't do her work) or if she is quite dependable and can work on her own.

On the flip side, when women need to be directive and call the shots, they often shy away from "throwing around their power" even though the employee may need them to do so. The employee may test the limits to determine whether this manager is going to behave like a leader.

The key to being a great leader is the ability to be strategic rather than remaining on automatic pilot. You need to choose your styles including being directive and showing your power when appropriate, even if it feels unnatural to you. The following situations will guide you in honing these leadership skills.

1. The Situation:
You're unsure what leadership style to use.

You are a supervisor in the technical support division of a large utility company. Your organization is highly unionized and requires that you give all employees equal treatment. You have two stellar employees and consider yourself very lucky. They're dependable and do a great job technically without being monitored. Next week, a new employee—one who lacks experience in technical support—is transferring into your department from maintenance.

To be fair, you decide you'll have to give the new employee the same latitude you've given your two veterans. Is this the best approach?

The Solution:

If you're managing all of your employees the same way, you're probably managing some of them inappropriately. Whether or not you're in a union shop, to be an effective leader you should use different styles with different employees.

Since you don't yet know where your new employee stands, start out slowly and monitor her closely until you have assessed her technical skills and her ability to carry out the job on her own. Establish clear expectations and have her report to you weekly on her progress. You may be setting her up for failure if you allow her a great deal of latitude without the safety of structure. Besides, she will resent you if you give her freedom at first and then take it away. It's best to provide each employee with the structure and guidance he or she needs to do the job well.

Rule: Fit your leadership style to the employee.

---

2. The Situation:
Your employee doesn't perform as expected.

You run a construction firm and have just hired a new administrative assistant. During the interview you made it clear that you expected Roy to be dependable and do an excellent job. He has been working for you for a month now, and you are irritated because he's behind in the filing, he types carelessly, and he doesn't proactively solve problems on his own but turns to you instead. When others in the company ask him to do work, he resists and they end up doing it themselves.

You feel like sitting Roy down and reading him the riot act, but you wonder if that's the right approach to take.

The Solution:

People need to be told exactly what's expected of them. To manage them well, you must explain in advance the quality and quantity of what they're supposed to produce, as well as what the end product should look like. Effective managers set clear and reachable goals for their employees. This provides new employees with the structure they need so they understand how to be successful. They know where the goal line is.

The problem is not with Roy; it is with you. Vague phrases like "doing an excellent job" or "being dependable" are unattached to specific behaviors. Roy may have been doing what he thought was a good job, but that may be different from your idea of a good job.

Instead of reprimanding him, sit down with him and set out some very clear goals that are specific, measurable, reachable, and time-bound. For example, you might tell him that he must answer phones within two rings, complete all filing within 24 hours, and turn in documents that are 99 percent free of typos. You should also make clear to him who else in the company he is to support. (He may resist working for others because he doesn't know you expect it of him. In fact, he may believe that the other employees are simply trying to push their work off on him.)

When you make the goals clear, you set yourself up for a smooth performance appraisal down the road. You can evaluate your employee based on how well he has reached these predetermined goals. If Roy has done his job poorly, he won't think that you are picking on him; it will be clear to both of you that he has chosen to be mediocre. In other words, you won't be the bad guy.

Rule: Set clear and reachable goals for performance with your employees.

---

3. The Situation:
You're overwhelmed by a new position offered you.

You are the articles editor of a national women's magazine. The publisher calls you into her office to ask if you'd be interested in becoming managing editor. Your first response is to point out how frightened and inexperienced you are by saying, "Wow. That would be a big responsibility. I'm not sure I could do it. I don't know about the fiction department. I have no experience with layout. With the increased hours, I'd have to manage my child care differently. Let me think about it."

After leaving this meeting, you wonder if you've blown a valuable opportunity. What should you do?

The Solution:

Women often feel uncomfortable taking on leadership positions. This is due in part to growing up in a nonhierarchical culture and to the fact that women focus on their weaknesses rather than their strengths.

You can be sure that if you don't take this coveted position, someone else will, much to your chagrin and resentment. This might be a prime opportunity for you to practice a little risk taking. Everything you know about your job up to this point you learned by doing. That's how you're going to learn what you need to know in order to be an effective managing editor.

Go back to your publisher and thank her for asking you about the position. You could say, "I've thought it over, and I believe that I could learn what I need to know in any of the areas in which I don't yet have skills. We have a lot of good employees in these areas who have been handling the work up to this point. If you're still interested in me, I want to take on the challenge."

Rule: Embrace power and leadership positions.

---

4. The Situation:
Your male employees challenge you.

You are one of the first women to be appointed manager of a large grocery store. When you got the job, you knew that the corporate office believed this market didn't have the profit margin it should, given the area's demographics. To get input from long-term employees who you believe have many good ideas, you have started to involve them in problem solving and decision making.

You've noticed, however, that some of your male employees are now going over your head to your manager and ignoring you when you give them specific directions. You've even overheard comments that you're a weak manager. Your authority is eroding. What's happening here?

The Solution:

Men expect their leaders to assert authority because that's how a hierarchy works. If the leader doesn't exercise her power, male employees may perceive her as weak and ineffectual.

You know from your own experience that this store has been run in a hierarchical mode. Your employees are used to taking orders from above. If you abruptly switch to a collaborative style, you may be creating too much change too quickly. Gradually introduce your employees to participation.

Still, it can be a good idea to involve employees in decision making and problem solving because you can capture their brain power. They often see problems more clearly than those farther up the hierarchy. Besides, if your employees know they can contribute to solving problems, they will be more motivated to carry out the decisions and make the ideas work.

On the other hand, you must also make it clear that you *can* make the decisions, but you choose to work collaboratively because you believe in your employees and their abilities. If you still find them sidestepping you or failing to carry out specific directions, you must assert your authority and monitor them closely.

Given how few women are general managers of grocery stores, it's also likely that these men have never worked for a woman. They may be resistant for a variety of reasons: They believe a man should have gotten the job; it doesn't "look" right to have a woman boss; women can't really manage. Consequently, they'll probably test you just to see if you're really the boss.

Rule: When in a leadership position, assert your authority, especially around male employees.

---

5. The Situation:
Your women employees want to talk over your decisions.

You've been hired as the executive director of a nonprofit agency that provides support for individuals with debilitating chronic illnesses. Your employees care very much about the services they provide, but the business end of the organization is a mess: The fund-raising is weak, service to clients is inconsistent, and office routines are inefficient and disorganized. The board of directors has made it clear to you that they want you to turn the situation around pronto.

You have taken the reins well in hand and have been issuing directives about how each of these problems will now be addressed. Although you know that what you're doing will work, you are getting backlash from your employees who had been intimately involved in all decisions in the past. Do you stay the course and continue going it alone?

The Solution:

It's great to collaborate with employees when it's appropriate. On the other hand, if you are having major problems and need to find quick solutions, collaboration won't work best. You must take charge of the situation despite your employees' momentary disgruntlement.

The first step is to make clear to your personnel the problems the organization is facing. They need to perceive the obstacles with the same intensity as you do. You may wish to share with them the agency's financial status and then add, "I've made some immediate short-term decisions about what should be done. I hope I can count on your support."

Without such an explanation, you may simply look like a dictator, especially to your female employees. If they perceive you as barging in and throwing around directives, ignoring them for no good reason, they will feel resentful at your sudden intrusion. They'll believe that the problem is really you and not the difficult situation you all find yourselves in.

Once you're out of the emergency stage and your employees demonstrate their competence and commitment to this new strategy, you can begin involving them in the decision making, as appropriate.

**Rule: If you need a quick solution, take charge.
Don't collaborate.**

---

6. The Situation:
The higher-ups don't see you as "leadership material."

You've never considered yourself power hungry, but you're tired of watching promotions go to people who aren't as good as you are. You've heard through the grapevine that you're not perceived as being leadership material and that you're not corporate enough.

You're disturbed by this characterization since everyone acknowledges that you do excellent work and always help others. How can you move ahead?

The Solution:

Power is neither good nor bad. Like money, it's what you do with it that's important. In the corporate hierarchy, power is the ability to get things done. Yet for women, seeking power may seem like dirty work. Nevertheless, in order to be successful you need to be powerful, but you don't have to hurt other people in the process. If you're perceived as being weak, however, others will deny you opportunities to demonstrate what you can accomplish.

Whether you're power hungry or not, start presenting yourself as a powerful person in order to reach your goals. You might ask a mentor for some pointers. Also, notice who gets promoted and why: How do they speak, what do they wear, with whom do they have lunch, how often do they meet with the boss, what do they talk about during those meetings? There are myriad ways to exude a powerful image. See chapter 6, Power Talk, and chapter 7, Power Moves, for some useful suggestions.

Rule: Be powerful to be successful.

---

7. The Situation:
You want to be powerful and still maintain your femininity.

You've just been elected to the city council. Learning the ropes of this quasi-legal system has been difficult. During meetings, your male colleagues often raise their voices or pound on the table. You're not sure this will work for you. You don't want to start acting like a man, but you are aware that when you're polite and ladylike and smile a lot your colleagues ignore your ideas. Is there a happy medium?

The Solution:

You were right to be concerned about behaving like your male colleagues. The double standard still prevails; a woman simply cannot mimic males' behavior. Women are judged by women's rules: They may speak loudly but not yell; they may make definitive gestures but not pound. A man may shout, pound his fists on the table, or throw things, and it is all taken in stride. If a woman does these things, she will most likely be labeled a "crazy bitch," if not worse. If you act like a man, it will most assuredly cost you in some way.

Be strategic and recognize how far you can push the bounds of acceptable behavior for women. There are times when it would be appropriate for you to be warm and expressive. On other occasions you will want to be more assertive.

Communicate your powerfulness to others using those behaviors acceptable for women such as:

- lack of facial expression
- a firm voice
- open posture
- interrupting to make your point

Bear in mind that certain behaviors are virtually never acceptable for women, including yelling or screaming, pounding on the table, or throwing things.

Rule: Observe the feminine boundaries of power.

---

8. The Situation:
You're offered a big assignment for which you feel unprepared.

You work in marketing and coordinate national ad campaigns in a midsize toy company. Your boss has mentioned to you that the position of budget manager has opened up in finance. She has asked you if you would be interested in this lateral move. She thinks highly of you and believes this would be a great growth opportunity.

You're floored by the prospect. Although you had coordinated some budget activities for the company in the previous year, you don't hold an MBA, and your overall experience with finance is limited to your department's needs. You don't feel ready to take on such a large responsibility, yet you don't want this great opportunity to pass you by. What should you do?

The Solution:

Boys learn in childhood that the way to intimidate other players is to act as if they feel confident and to never let their weak side show. Many senior executives have found themselves in the same position in their careers: They were asked to do something they didn't know how to do, yet they took on the challenge anyway. Men call this risk taking.

Moreover, organizations often groom individuals for senior positions by moving them into jobs in which they have no technical background. How quickly they catch on lets senior management know that these individuals can handle difficult situations. Research has shown that taking such significant career risks (even if the move is lateral) is three times more important for women's success than it is for men's.

This may be the opportunity to move ahead in your career. Here's how to do it:

1. Don't go into a litany about why you're not ready for this position. Women call this being honest, but it will undermine others' belief in your ability to carry out the job.

2. Get some information about the position, its requirements, and the skills of those who would be working under you. You'll have to convince the VP of finance (to whom you would be reporting) that you're capable of handling the job. Without this information, you will be unable to do so.

3. Assess what skills you would need to do the job well. Do you have these skills? If some are lacking, you must be able to fill in the gaps fast enough to be a successful budget manager.

4. Take a deep breath and go for it!

Rule: Make it up and act as if you know.

$$6$$

Power Talk

O ur speech patterns are subtle and communicate much more than we may be aware of. Every day we unconsciously convey our attitudes toward leadership, power, teamwork, and relationships through the words we use.

Women flatten the hierarchical structure linguistically. For example, if a woman receives a compliment from another woman about a new outfit, she's apt to reply, "Oh, this old thing. I got it on sale three years ago," so as not to be better than her friend.

That can work well in the culture of women, but when women do this with men, it creates problems for them. For example, if a male colleague compliments your work and you deprecate it by saying, "Gee, I just lucked out," he's apt to dismiss your abilities and contributions and see you as beneath him in the hierarchy.

Furthermore, women are comfortable talking about personal relationships. A woman can meet another woman at a party and know her life history and most intimate aspirations in five minutes. On the other hand, men in that same setting are more likely to make small talk about impersonal issues such as "the big game" and may even banter with each other verbally as a way of saying "I like you." The following situations and solutions will help you identify verbal patterns that might be working to your disadvantage and substitute more powerful communications.

1. The Situation:
Men tune you out during a meeting.

You work in the marketing department of a power-tool company. Your boss has asked you to put together a presentation for the executives on whether it's better to sell a new product retail or through distributors. This is an opportunity for you to demonstrate how well you can analyze the industry and come up with a marketing strategy.

You have put a lot of work into this report and have written a small tome on the subject. As the meeting begins, you start to explain in detail the pros and cons of each of the options. About 15 minutes into the presentation, you notice that the executives' eyes are beginning to glaze over. Where have you gone wrong, and what can you do about it?

The Solution:

In the female culture it would be presumptuous for a woman to tell others what to do without first explaining her rationale. Women give the thought process behind their decision before they state their conclusion. Men skip the explanation and cut to the chase. When women provide the background before getting to the bottom line, men perceive them as being too talkative. The rationale sounds like a waste of time to them.

To salvage your presentation, stop giving the background and jump right into the meat of your proposal. You might say, for example, "We have a variety of options, but let me get to the bottom line. I'm recommending that we…"

In the future share a few facts that underlie what you have to say, but get to the point quickly. You can fill in the details later. For your presentation, you might have said, "The other products that we sell retail are in trouble financially and our competitors have been successful using distributors. *I'm going to recommend that we also use distributors for our new product.* Let me give you the numbers." Then you can explain how you arrived at your conclusion.

**Rule: Men are goal oriented in their communication.
Get to the bottom line quickly.**

---

2. The Situation:
Your boss turns cool.

You used to have a great relationship with your boss. You joked around together, went out to lunch, and shared the latest company scuttlebutt. But lately Jack seems cold toward you. When you ask him how his vacation plans for Mexico are going, he just gives you a clipped "Fine."

You feel something has happened to your relationship. Jack has stopped asking for your opinion at meetings. He now sends other managers elsewhere to get answers rather than to you and assigns you less challenging work than he previously had. You wonder if Jack no longer trusts you. You feel there may a problem in the relationship. You'd like to talk about it, but you're unsure how to broach the subject without putting him on the defensive.

The Solution:

You're right to be concerned about Jack's change of behavior. It might indicate that he has lost confidence in your performance. You have identified the issue as a problem within the relationship. But this topic is a bit too personal for a man who grew up in a culture in which relationship activities are not valued and never discussed.

Girls talk very intimately with their best friends about their relationship. This is enjoyable and continues to be so for women. Boys rarely talk about how they're feeling; instead, they focus on what the team needs to do to get to the goal line. At work, it's often easy for women to talk about relationships, but men avoid it like the plague.

Switch the conversation to a mode with which Jack will be comfortable. You can say, for example, "I've noticed that I'm not getting the same assignments anymore, and I've been wondering if you think there's something lacking in my performance. Are there any areas in which I can improve?"

This will allow Jack to coach you. The conversation can stay focused on how to reach the goal line—an area in which he feels a lot more comfortable.

Rule: Talking over interpersonal issues may be uncomfortable for a man. Reframe them as content issues.

---

3. The Situation:
Your input is passed over during a meeting.

You are an architect for a large hotel chain. Your organization is about to launch a new division of hotels geared to the business traveler. You believe that the company has made mistakes in the past by failing to solicit input from consumers. You feel it would be imperative at this point to conduct surveys and even focus groups, making potential hotel users an integral part of the design and development of this new division.

However, even though you've aired your concerns and recommendations with your male colleagues in advance, at a meeting to discuss the development of the new division, your input is simply passed over as other people give their ideas on how the hotels should be designed. How do you get others to listen to you?

The Solution:

In meetings, men indicate how much they believe in their ideas by persisting with their point of view, despite interruptions. This indicates their commitment to their plan. Women are used to taking turns and are more likely to divide the time equally. They may assess that there are five people at the meeting. They will take their "fair share" of the airtime and then let others speak.

Dominating the meeting with your ideas about customer involvement is the best way to show this group of men how committed you think the company should be to this concept. If the others ignore your plan, you must bring it up repeatedly. When interrupted, keep talking. This may feel pushy and aggressive, because to behave in this way with women would be perceived as being insensitive and bossy. Just keep in mind that you are a competitor here, slugging it out for your idea. If you don't fight for it, the others will think that you don't care about it and that it probably wasn't much of an idea to begin with.

Rule: Hold the floor in a meeting to signal how important you think your idea is.

---

4. The Situation:
You cringe at how you're introduced.

You are the vice principal in charge of counseling at a large urban junior high school. At a school district meeting, your boss, the principal, introduces you to Vincent, the county superintendent of guidance, by saying, "This is Charlene. She's one of the sweetest people you'll ever get to know. Everyone loves her. She's always ready to lend a helping hand."

Inside you're cringing. Jeff has made you sound like Rebecca of Sunnybrook Farm. How do you repair the damage without making you or him look bad?

The Solution:

Vincent is forming an image of you at this very moment. Be watchful of the impression you have made by the time he walks away; in the future, when your name comes up for advancement opportunities, he will match this perception with whether he believes you can handle the increased responsibility. The qualities that matter in the big game relate to your ability to help the team reach the goal line. Your interpersonal skills may be peerless, but if Jeff's comments are not clarified, Vincent probably won't value your skills much.

You may want to turn the conversation away from your more "feminine" qualities and focus on your ability to implement effective programs. Deftly draw Vincent's attention to your achievements by saying lightheartedly, "Jeff, I'm so glad you told Vincent the kids love me, because there were times when we were implementing my program to reduce gang violence and eliminate graffiti that I didn't feel so loved!"

Rule: Be aware of others introducing or describing you in powerless ways and take steps to correct a powerless description.

---

5. The Situation:
Your introduction is nice but weak.

You find yourself at a cocktail party and the ubiquitous question arises: "And what do you do?"

You talk about your position in an outplacement organization: "I work with individuals who have lost their jobs. I help them identify their strengths and develop a plan to find a new job." Although you think your work is important, clearly your conversation partner does not, as his eyes scan the room searching for the next potential contact.

The Solution:

Because men live their lives in hierarchies, when you introduce yourself they will be assessing your power relative to theirs. What you have achieved and the clout that you wield will make you powerful in their eyes.

It may be too difficult to repair your image in the eyes of this individual. However, in future contacts you can resolve to communicate your power and position as you introduce yourself. In fact, you might invoke the "royal 'We,'" as many men do, investing yourself with the power of your whole organization. You might say, for example, "I'm with Acme, an outplacement corporation. We work with Fortune 500 companies providing services to laid-off or terminated executives. Acme is the fastest-growing outplacement company in this region. We have $20 million in revenues."

Stay away from statements about whom you *help*. They also undermine your power and influence.

Rule: In introducing yourself, focus on power and influence.

---

6. The Situation:
A male colleague refers to women as "girls."

You're talking with a colleague about a tight situation he had been in when he says, "I'm so pleased with the help I got from the girls in office services."

You feel it is inappropriate for Phil to refer to these women as girls, but you don't quite know how to straighten him out. What do you do?

The Solution:

You're right in assessing that Phil is inappropriately diminishing the power of the women who work in office services. The research is very clear that our society views "girls" as lazy, weak, and inconsiderate. Although we conjure up an image of "ladies" as people who are beautiful and tasteful, in actuality the term is reserved for unfamiliar, low-status females. The term *woman* consistently garners the most favorable ratings and is used in practice for the most respectable of females as a term of power.

You'd like to raise Phil's consciousness, but to confront him directly may cause him to become defensive and resistant to changing his language. You have at least two options:

1. *The Juxtaposition Strategy.* Use the word *woman* in the next sentence, as in, "Yes, those women consistently do a great job." If after several attempts that doesn't work, you might consider using the second option.

2. *The Sledgehammer Method.* If this colleague is a peer or lower in the organization, you might say, "Phil, they're lucky to have an opportunity to work with a boy like you." If this individual is your boss or a senior executive, you may need to temper your tactic. In this case, you might say, "They couldn't have done it without the boys in shipping."

Rule: Call yourself and other female colleagues women, not girls or ladies.

---

7. The Situation:
The plumber calls you "honey."

You're talking to the plumber about the problem you've been having with your hot water heater. He asks you, "When did it start acting up like this, honey?"

You grit your teeth and reply, "Yesterday."

He follows up with, "Well, sweetie, has this happened before?"

When you say no, he continues, "Look, sugar, I don't have the parts with me to repair it today."

You're at the boiling point. You want to lash out. What do you say?

The Solution:

You're right in identifying these as inappropriate diminutive terms of affection. Use of these expressions often signals that in a man's eyes you are powerless. Indeed, these words may even indicate that the man believes you are a potential sexual liaison.

The most assertive thing to do is simply say, "I prefer to be called Pamela." This isn't an attack, and it doesn't indicate that he is wrong. You're simply stating your preference. But I must admit, when the situation becomes too much to tolerate, responding with "Well, baby-cakes, I'd appreciate your getting it fixed as soon as possible" usually does the trick.

**Rule: Notice epithets like "honey," "baby," or "sweetie."
If you feel uncomfortable with the affectionate term,
deal with it assertively.**

---

8. The Situation:
Your ideas are negated.

You and your colleague Chuck have been put in charge of the office redesign. You've had your initial meeting and you've been mulling over what the two of you have tentatively decided.

At the beginning of the next meeting, you say to Chuck, "I've been thinking about the design we worked on last time. This may be a stupid idea but I thought we might visit some recently remodeled offices. I sort of thought this might help us avoid some of the potential problems, you know?"

Chuck answers, "No, let's get this done as soon as possible. It's going to take too long to traipse around town."

You don't understand why he dismissed your ideas out of hand.

The Solution:

To encourage and include others' opinions in their flat-structure discussion, women will use the following:

+ verbal hedges such as "maybe," "some," "could be," "a little bit," "kind of," and "sort of"

+ disclaimers such as "I might be wrong but..." and "I'm not sure of this, however..."

+ tag questions like "you know?," "OK?," and "all right?"

To men, these expressions sound as if the woman hasn't a clue as to what she's doing and probably needs a man to give her some direction. While these expressions might be effective in including women in discussions, men hear them as an indication of incompetence.

When working with men, be aware of and avoid using verbal hedges, disclaimers, and tag questions. Compare the former statement with the following: "I've been mulling over the design we worked on last time. We'd benefit a great deal by looking at other recently remodeled offices. It'll allow us to learn from others' mistakes."

Rule: Don't sabotage yourself verbally with men:

+ **Shun hedges when you speak.**
+ **Avoid ending statements with question marks or tag questions.**
+ **Refrain from prefacing your statement with diminishing comments.**

---

9. The Situation:
PMS makes you cranky.

Your colleague Jeremy stops by to ask you why he hasn't received the report you promised him today. You snap, "I'll get to you when I can. I can't do everything at once."

He throws up his hands, says "OK," and walks out.

You feel badly because Jeremy is a valued co-worker. PMS is driving your foul mood here, so you go to him and say, "I'm sorry I snapped at you. It's just this PMS again."

He nods knowingly.

You think you've put the situation to rest. But will there be any other repercussions later?

The Solution:

Women see PMS or other menstrual issues as a normal part of life and of no particular consequence. Men, not having this experience, view it as foreign. They perceive a woman in the clutches of PMS as somewhat out of control. Consequently, they may not want her on their team, since they believe she may not come through when they need her to. They may attribute her emotional responses to menstrual or menopausal symptoms even if those responses are valid and to the point. It's best to leave bodily functions out of discussions with male colleagues.

It was appropriate for you to apologize for snapping at Jeremy, but you didn't have to mention PMS. You could simply have said, "I'm sorry I barked at you this morning. I'm having a rough day."

Rule: Never bring up your period, PMS, or menopause among male co-workers.

---

10. The Situation:
Friendly men are suddenly rude.

You're the marketing manager of a large household products firm. You, along with managers of a variety of divisions from across the country, attend an annual company meeting.

You walk up to some colleagues whom you've met at similar gatherings in prior years. Ben, who works in R&D, and Rick, an engineering manager, are laughing. As you approach, you hear Rick say to Ben, "Where do you guys come up with those ideas? Your beard-and-sandal set needs to come back to reality once in a while. Why don't you stop by my operation and check out what goes on in the real world?"

"If you didn't have a bunch of monkeys working for you," Ben replies, "you wouldn't have problems with the new design."

"Well, at least I've got monkeys instead of the rodents in your department," Rick fires back.

They turn to you, laughing, and say, "Oh, look, here's Gloria. Now we get to hear about the latest harebrained scheme from marketing."

Do these guys hate you? Do they hate each other? How are you going to respond?

The Solution:

Boys don't share intimacies. As a result, one of the ways that they communicate fondness for one another and negotiate position in the hierarchy is through verbal bantering. If you observe two young boys playing, you'll likely hear the following:

Tommy: "You look like a frog."

Jimmy: "Oh yeah? Well, you look like a Tyrannosaurus rex."

Translation: I like you.

If girls carried on in this way, it would damage their relationships.

Rick and Ben are bonding. They are playfully telling each other that they have a good relationship. They have turned to you and have included you in this bonding activity. If you become insulted or distance yourself from them, they will read your behavior as meaning you don't care about your relationship with them. It may be helpful to add the new skill of verbal bantering to your game strategy.

A possible response to their playful gibes: "If you guys would get

your noses out of your knobs and wires, you might realize that marketing is really running this company." Be sure to laugh and smile as you
say this so they understand you're playing their game.

Rule: Identify and participate in verbal bantering.

7

Power Moves

◆◆◆

I n much the same way as verbal communication, our nonverbal cues send messages about how much power we have, how confident we feel, how aggressive we are in a discussion, and whether we are comfortable with or intimidated by others.

Some nonverbal messages are interpreted differently by women than they are by men. Gestures as simple as nodding your head or changing your stance when talking with another can convey unintended messages that may be completely misread.

Not surprisingly, women's cues in general indicate sharing power and enhancing relationships. Men's cues often demonstrate power in the hierarchy and are aimed at negotiating position. The following situations and solutions will teach you useful Hardball power moves.

1. The Situation:
The management committee gangs up on you
to criticize your proposal.

For the past several months you've been working on restructuring your department in a furniture manufacturing company. You've involved the employees in this process and they have worked in subcommittees to come up with recommendations. All of you have pulled together the new ideas to make sure that you can continue to deliver good service to your clients quickly and efficiently.

Your boss has been pleased with the process and the outcome of what you're proposing. Today, you are presenting the proposed new structure to the senior management committee of your organization. Their approval is the last hurdle you must clear before you can implement your plan.

At the meeting, you present the design and begin to explain the rationale behind it. For reasons you can't fathom, one individual on the management committee begins taking potshots at it. Others join the fray. Soon it seems they're not interested in hearing what you have to say. You wonder if you're contributing to the fact that they're all piling on.

The Solution:

The first rule of swimming with the sharks is not to bleed. If men sense that an opponent is weak, they begin to attack.

When under assault, we often signal our vulnerability with nonverbal cues. We may pull in our bodies and get small to protect ourselves. The converse—pulling up and spreading out—sends the message that the attacks aren't getting through. Also, in our culture, it is normal to tilt one's head when listening to someone. But if you tilt yours during speech, you indicate insecurity and powerlessness.

Finally, a particular smile is frequently associated with subordinate status. This may be an inborn trait. Other primates use this grin when they're feeling intimidated. It indicates submission and fear. Among humans, the smile is a sign of appeasement and friendship, but a tinge of anxiety can remain. Think back to your fifth grade classroom when the teacher shouted, "And wipe that grin off your face!" to a child she had just scolded.

Of course, smiling is fine if you're happy or you find a situation funny. But the please-don't-attack-me-anymore smile occurs in situations in which you feel uncomfortable or frightened and indicates powerlessness.

If you're in a difficult or unpleasant situation, and are aware that you're displaying this type of body language, you most assuredly are communicating to the management committee that you are vulnerable. This fuels their attack. Keep your face impassive and your head upright. In addition, be aware of your posture. If you're sitting, throw your shoulders back and put your arms on the armrests of your chair. If you're standing, keep your shoulders back and make sure your gestures are open. Don't cross your arms. Fill the space with your presence. (Also see situation #10, chapter 2, on what to do when attacked by a group.)

Rule: When under attack, keep a stone face and make yourself big. Don't shrink, tilt your head, or display the please-don't-attack-me-anymore smile.

---

2. The Situation:
A male co-worker thinks you've turned on him.

You're a doctor in a large pediatric practice. Your colleague, Marc, came to you yesterday to talk about his belief that the office would be more profitable in a different neighborhood.

You listen intently, nodding from time to time, to let Marc know that you've heard what he has to say. Later, at a meeting, you voice your reservations about his idea. You feel the relocation costs would outweigh any benefits.

After the meeting, Mark comes storming into your office, claiming you turned on him. Since you never said that you agreed with him or would support him, you're surprised at his reaction. How do you clear the air?

The Solution:

When women are listening to someone, they nod as a way of saying "I hear you. You've got the floor. Keep going." These nods do not necessarily mean "I agree with you." Men nod when they are in agreement. As a result, a man may believe that a woman's nods and noises mean that she agrees with him.

Conversely, women often misinterpret a listening man's lack of nods as a sign that he has simply tuned out, when in fact he may be listening intently. He may simply disagree, and that's why he is not nodding.

Marc took your nods to mean that you were behind his suggestion. That was not the message you meant to send, and therefore Marc feels that you've betrayed him and can't be trusted.

To patch things up, tell Marc, "I understand that you were counting on my support in the meeting this morning. I don't remember telling you that I was behind your idea. To tell you the truth, the more I thought about it, the more I had reservations. I'm sorry if there was some confusion about my position."

An ounce of prevention is worth a pound of cure. It's best to be cautious about nodding your head as you're listening to an unacceptable position. This could send the wrong signal to a man. If you just can't keep your head still, verbally explain your reservations so that your colleague doesn't get the wrong message.

Rule: Nods and assenting noises may tell a man you agree when you don't, so pay attention to your gestures.

---

3. The Situation:
You're unsure when you should shake a woman's hand.

Colleagues at your husband's office are holding a private dinner party. Jerry, your husband, introduces you to his co-workers and their spouses. You don't want to make a faux pas. In this social setting, should you shake hands with the men? With the women? With everyone?

The Solution:

Men in our culture are brought up to shake hands; women are not. As a result, women can be confused about when they should shake hands. This becomes doubly difficult when the person to whom one is introduced is a woman.

When it comes to shaking hands, you have only two options: to shake or not to shake. It's better to err on the side of overshaking. People may complain, "She didn't shake my hand and should have," but rarely would you hear someone say, "She shook my hand and should not have."

Shake everyone's hand. To shake with the men and not with the women sends the signal that women are different or even less important.

What about other situations? Say you find yourself in one of the following:

+ You met the individual yesterday but you see her or him again just before a big meeting.
+ A colleague introduces you to her secretary.
+ You know the individual but haven't seen him or her in a while.

Here too, it's best to err on the side of overshaking.

When you shake hands, avoid the "dead fish" grip. Grasp the other hand firmly, web to web, and wrap your fingers around it. Look the individual in the eye. Be wary: during interviews, many job opportunities have been lost because of the dead-fish handshake.

Rule: Initiate the firm handshake.
---

4. The Situation:
A conflict worsens.

You're a staff nurse. You've worked with Dr. Specter for several years. He likes to have his way and tends to get volatile when questioned by a nurse. He tells you to give a particular medication to Mrs. Dutton. Given the other medications she's taking, you're concerned that she'll have an adverse reaction. You're fortunate enough to work at a hospital in which administration will back you up in situations like this. And so you express your doubts to Dr. Specter.

He doesn't take kindly to your intervention. "I *am* the doctor," he says huffily. "And where did *you* go to medical school?"

You become incensed. You wag your finger at him and say, "As the nurse, I'm this patient's advocate. I'm concerned about the interaction of her medications."

Dr. Specter takes off down the hallway, yelling, "I'm going to talk to the administrator about nurses not following orders in this hospital."

You wonder how you could have handled this situation better.

The Solution:

Pointing and wagging a finger is a power move. (Parents often point and wag at their children.) In tense, conflictual situations, pointing can inflame the interaction, particularly if the other person is concerned about his power.

Dr. Specter is already feeling as if you're challenging his authority. What's worse, he comes from the medical culture, which is highly hierarchical. Although your concerns and resistance may be quite appropriate, you need to communicate in a way that will give a win-win outcome. You might say, for instance, "I'm as concerned as you are that Mrs. Dutton gets her meds. I'll be glad to do some quick research to find out about drug interactions. I'll get that to you right away."

Pointing and wagging a finger is a sure way to send Dr. Specter into orbit. In this as well as other potentially explosive situations, make sure that you interact without using this gesture.

Rule: Don't point at others in conflictual
or sensitive situations.

---

5. The Situation:
You betray your anxiety.

You had a bad relationship with your previous boss and got fired over a clash of styles. Now you're out interviewing and you've noticed that when you're asked why you're presently unemployed, you become very uncomfortable. You know the interview is over because of how you're handling this difficult question. What should you watch for when you're explaining your current state of employment?

The Solution:

Whenever we feel anxious or uneasy, we naturally tend to comfort ourselves by rubbing, patting, or scratching ourselves. Next time you're stuck in a traffic jam, look at others around you. You'll observe men touching their beards, women stroking their hair or faces, and so forth.

Furthermore, when we're interacting with others and the situation feels too close—we've been asked a sensitive question, we're embarrassed by a situation, we feel uncomfortable with an individual—we break eye contact as a way of giving ourselves some distance.

You can predict that your interviewers are going to ask you why you're presently unemployed. Come up with a good explanation of what happened. Practice your statement so that you feel comfortable saying it. When actually delivering it during your interview, keep your hands off your body and maintain what is normal eye contact for you. If it is just too uncomfortable to look the person in the eye, look at the bridge of his or her nose. No one will know the difference. (See situation #1 in this chapter for other important power moves when you're put in an uncomfortable position.)

Rule: Avoid rubbing, patting, or scratching yourself in uncomfortable situations. Continue to maintain eye contact.

---

6. The Situation:
You feel overpowered in a discussion.

You're in charge of travel arrangements for a national dance touring company. Jason, the male lead in the troupe, was mighty displeased when he heard about the hotel accommodations you made in Paris. As you sit at your desk, he barges into your office, ranting and raving about your lack of concern for the needs of the talent.

As he stands over you, talking loudly and gesticulating, you begin to feel as if you're in the power-down position in this interaction. What can you do to level the playing field?

The Solution:

When we physically and literally have to talk up to someone, we feel less powerful or confident than when we're at equal eye level with them. If you find yourself in a situation such as this, figure out how you can get yourself on the same eye level as Jason. You have a few options.

The first is to say, "I'm really glad you came to see me about this. Here, take a seat so that we can talk about it." If he won't sit down, then it behooves you to stand up. Unfortunately, this is not as effective because most women are shorter than most men, but it's better than the height disparity between sitting and standing.

If Jason were to corner you in the hallway, you might consider saying to him, "I really want to hear what you have to say about this. Why don't we go into my office and sit down to talk about it." Head for the nearest chairs.

If you're dealing with a bully on the phone, stand up and pace as you speak. (You'll probably need a longer phone cord.) This will give you an additional sense of power.

Rule: Maneuver your way out of having to look up.

---

7. The Situation:
You're perceived as being aggressive.

You're a dentist attending a regional conference. You are conversing with Gil, a colleague and fellow board member from another city. Although you've always enjoyed seeing Gil, you feel that he isn't really interested in talking with you. He seems more focused on watching the others at the gathering. You try to engage him in a conversation but don't seem to connect.

You are completely floored the next day to hear that Gil was surprised at how aggressive you've become when he spoke with you at the meeting. What's going on here?

The Solution:

When women interact with other women, they face each other directly. When men interact with men, they tend to stand shoulder to shoulder and talk to the empty space in front of them. Typically, men only face each other directly during conflict situations. In fact, the most aggressive stance for men is face-to-face with hands on hips.

When interacting with a member of the opposite sex, we try to position our bodies in the most familiar (and thus comfortable) position for our gender.

You may have felt that Gil had disengaged himself from your conversation because he had simply tried to get into a more comfortable stance, turning his body sideways to yours. You might have interpreted his shift as an indication of his disinterest. When you tried to remedy the situation by attempting to face him directly, he might have perceived your movement as a sign of aggression.

In the future, let your male colleagues adjust their stance while you stay planted. Mentally remind yourself that their position does not indicate disengagement, but rather is the most comfortable way for them to stand.

Rule: Don't adjust your body axis to face head-on when talking to a man. He may perceive you as being aggressive.

---

8. The Situation:
You decline the fancy office.

You're elated to discover that you've been promoted to director of plant operations. Your predecessor had a well-appointed office with a drop-dead view.

The office manager brings you the catalog so that you can order your new furniture for your large office. "Thanks," you tell her, "but I've decided not to move into that office because it's too far away from my team." (It's down two hallways and around a corner.) You're staying in your old office, which is comparable to those of the managers who now report to you.

Your boss has heard about your decision and has stopped by to ask you if there's a problem with your new office. "The other office is just fine," you explain, "but I want to stay with my group."

He raises one eyebrow and walks out. What does the raised eyebrow mean?

The Solution:

Women often look at their physical work surroundings functionally. If the chair is comfortable, the lighting adequate, and the office is close to people they have to talk with frequently, they're satisfied.

The hierarchical culture of men dictates that people display how much power they have so that others within that culture know how to interact appropriately with them (that is, with whom one must be deferential or who one can challenge).

If you remain in your old office, you will send a confusing message to your male colleagues and employees. Your colleagues will have a difficult time accepting you as an equal member of the team because you've chosen to stay in a low-status territory. And some of your male employees may challenge your authority because visually you look just like a peer to them.

There are, however, some advantages to interacting frequently with your team. You might consider calling two spots your office or maintaining a desk in your original territory. Given a particular meeting or piece of work, you can strategically choose which is the better place for you to conduct your business.

Rule: You may not really care about the trappings of power, but they still signal how much power you have. Take them on.

---

9. The Situation:
You lose an important client because of your choice of entertainment venue.

Your company provides insurance products to corporations. You frequently have to take clients, generally directors of human resources, out to lunch or dinner.

You are entertaining Harvey, the director of human resources in a midsize tool company, at one of the finest restaurants in the area. You did some research to make sure that it was among the best, because this company is an important client that you don't want to lose. You know that the competition has been in to talk to Harvey.

During lunch, all does not go smoothly. You sense that Harvey is uncomfortable. He keeps looking around the room and at his watch. When you part after lunch, things seem a bit strained, and later that week, Harvey seems more ambivalent about recommitting to your company's program.

What could have gone wrong? After all, you took him to the nicest place you could find.

The Solution:

Be sure that where you entertain Harvey is consistent with how he sees himself. It should be familiar territory for him. For example, if he's a short-sleeved-white-shirt, polyester-tie kind of guy, he might feel uncomfortable at an expensive French restaurant. He's used to tacos at the local Mexican joint. Sharpen your powers of observation. When Harvey shows up at your office, you will get a sense, given how he's dressed, as to where he'll feel at ease. You could even ask him what (or where) he likes to eat.

Also, you need to make sure that you're in tune with the culture of Harvey's organization, because you want to be seen as a quasi-member. All companies have cultures. They are reflected in how social activities occur: where the off-site meetings are called, the kind of food served, the required dress, and so on.

If Harvey's tool company runs "lean and mean" and caters meetings from the local deli, he may perceive your business as too high-priced if you lunch at an exclusive bistro. Conversely, if most of the company meetings are at the Ritz-Carlton and you take Harvey to your favorite hamburger stand, he may conclude that he's an unimportant client. If you're unsure of his company's culture, ask others who may be familiar with it.

Rule: Choose restaurants wisely.

10. The Situation:
Your boss invites you for drinks.

Your boss, George, is the director of real estate at a large international corporation. You're working late one Friday night when he and one of his peers stop by and ask if you want to join them for a drink. Everyone has had a high-stress week and you've closed some critical deals. You're the only person left in the office.

You go to the local watering hole and both men order doubles. What should you do?

The Solution:

Most organizations have an unwritten policy about alcohol consumption. In some cases it's one discreet glass of wine, and at the other end of the continuum the company adopts a "party hearty" atmosphere where the liquor flows freely.

That having been said, it's important to note that the high consumption rules don't apply to women. Women should not drink heavily in a work-related situation. They'll be seen as "loose" women who might even be sexually available.

Although a man may keep his private life to himself under most work circumstances, he will often share personal troubles about his wife, family, or job when intoxicated. This is comfortable "bonding talk" to a woman. She may even expect the relationship to be warmer back at the office on Monday as a result. Instead, however, she may find that the man ignores her. She now knows his weaknesses, and he may perceive her presence as dangerous. It's best to avoid these alcohol-induced conversations.

Don't order a double. Stick to a glass of wine—at the most two glasses will suffice. If George and his colleague start to get inebriated, you may be entering dangerous territory. Probably the best thing you can do is thank him for inviting you along, say, "I'll see you guys on Monday," and leave.

Rule: Observe your company's ethic regarding drinking, but also limit your intake. The double standard still does apply.

8

Making the Most
of Criticism and Praise

◆◆◆

B oys grow up receiving criticism constantly from the
coach who tells them that they run like a duck, hold
the bat wrong, or (the very worst) play like a girl.
They learn that criticism from the coach helps them
become better players. They don't relish the negative feedback, but they know that to move up in the hierarchy, they
must take it in, learn from it (thereby improving their
skills), and then move on. They learn to seek out criticism,
since they regard it as a means of improving their performance, yet they distance it from their sense of self.

Girls rarely receive that kind of comment or training
during their childhood. No one tells them to hold their
dolls straight, for example, or the right way to play school.
And so girls tend to hold criticism more personally and to
see it as targeting their entire being.

Women avoid criticism because of the great pain it
causes them. Moreover, they often assume that because
they receive positive comments from the powers-that-be,
they will be rewarded appropriately. Unfortunately, they
often miss what is unsaid: their superiors' hidden concerns,
agendas, and issues. For example, they may never even
dream that their interaction style or a sanctioned maternity leave may be a problem.

As professional women, however, we need to overcome
our aversion to criticism and view it as a source of valuable
information for career growth. Because we can't see ourselves the way others do, we must solicit critical input,
even if it's completely off base. Without it, we can't manage the perceptions others hold of us.

And because we are more likely to define ourselves
according to how others perceive us, when absorbing criti-

cism we give others too much power over our self-esteem and even our lives. Once we receive the criticism, we must also guard against it destroying us. We should not allow our internal dialogue to become negative; rather, we should use the information for what it's worth and then proceed with our lives.

Women are apt to make the playing field even. Consequently, we often dismiss praise; we don't want to seem better than others. In the process, we rob ourselves of the opportunity to further our position in the hierarchy. We should take a cue from our male counterparts and learn how to extend praise for the benefit of our careers. This chapter will help you learn from criticism and extend praise.

1. The Situation:
You're crushed by critical comments.

You're supervisor in matériel in a large, diversified company. You are interviewing for a job in another division because it's closer to your home and would cut down on your commuting time.

The interviewer, Neil, tells you after the interview is over that you probably don't have the job. He explains, "You are light on technical knowledge but also you seem to be a bit defensive, like you have a chip on your shoulder. You need to ask more questions. During our interview, you didn't seem interested in this division."

You leave the office devastated, in part because you know you didn't get the job, but primarily because of Neil's critical comments regarding your interviewing skills.

How do you handle this?

The Solution:

Although you may feel irreparably devastated, Neil has given you a wonderful opportunity to improve your interviewing skills. You need to identify what you were doing that caused Neil to believe you were defensive or uninterested in his division. Change those behaviors for the next interview. (You might even drop Neil a note, thanking him for being so candid with you.)

Once you have taken into account everything you can learn from this unpleasant situation, it's wise to take criticism for what it's worth and move on. That means dropping the whole subject. (See situation #3 on self-talk in this chapter.)

Rule: Use criticism as a tool for self-improvement.

2. The Situation:
You take criticism personally.

You're a reporter for a big-city newspaper. Your usual beat is the Women's Page, where you cover human interest stories. But Jonathan, your editor, has assigned you a hard-news report on a local murder. You do the best you can with it, giving the story a human twist, but Jonathan is displeased.

He comes by and hands your story back to you. "This report is junk," he says. "You ramble, the facts just aren't there, and it's way too soft." He turns and walks away.

You want to crawl under your desk. You doubt your abilities as a writer and wonder how you ever got a job at such a prestigious newspaper. In short, you now feel that you are stupid and inadequate and that you'll never write a decent story again. How can you pull out of this tailspin?

The Solution:

The boss was criticizing your report, not your existence. You need to focus on fixing the story. Take the opportunity to learn what you can from this experience and then drop it. Your boss's harsh words were not about who you are as a person. (See situation #3 on self-talk.)

Rule: Separate criticism of an act from your feelings about yourself as a person.

---

3. The Situation:
You put yourself down.

You've always been a top-rated performer. Six months ago, you got a new boss. From the beginning Joyce has not been satisfied with your performance. Nothing you do seems to be what she is looking for. This is hard enough on your ego, but soon you receive the ultimate blow: Joyce takes you out to lunch and informs you that you are being terminated.

The two weeks that follow are the most difficult of your life. You find the following negative statements running through your mind all day long:

- ◆ "I should have tried harder to please Joyce."
- ◆ "If I had asked more questions, maybe she would have given me more information."
- ◆ "I should have known better than to stay after she became my boss."
- ◆ "How dense can I be? Why didn't I see this coming?"
- ◆ "Maybe I'm not cut out for this kind of work."

You have to get ready to start interviewing, but whenever you look in the mirror you think nobody will want to hire someone who looks like such a loser.

What can you do to turn the situation around?

The Solution:

We all talk to ourselves. Sometimes that talk is positive:

- ◆ "This job is a piece of cake."
- ◆ "I'm going to shine on this project."
- ◆ "I really know what I'm doing."

Sometimes self-talk is negative, such as "What a stupid thing to do. I should have known better."

Self-talk isn't just words that ramble around in our brains; it physically impacts our behavior. If you tell yourself that you can't do something, in all likelihood you won't be able to. The converse is also true.

Self-talk is often unconscious. You need to hear it before you can change it. Start monitoring your internal monologue. If you hear yourself repeating negative statements, stop and replace the criticism with a positive remark. For example, if you tell yourself, "I should have tried harder to please Joyce," say instead, "I did everything I could to please her. Our personalities didn't jibe." Or, if you think, "Maybe I'm not cut out for this kind of work," replace it with "I've always been a top performer and I'll be a top performer again."

Some women find it helpful to wear a rubber band on their wrist and snap it every time negative thoughts intrude. This may seem bizarre, but it provides immediate and physical feedback and helps you to change negative self-talk quickly.

Rule: Transform negative self-talk into positive self-talk.

4. The Situation:
You don't know how seriously you should take some criticism.

You find yourself in the unfortunate circumstance of caring for your widowed mother, who is suffering from advanced cardiovascular disease. She has been seeing doctors with great frequency and has been in and out of the hospital often.

Because of her weakened state, you've taken it upon yourself to be her advocate. You're constantly questioning the physicians about the risks and benefits of the treatments they've prescribed, the medications, and the prognosis.

One day you overhear the nurses in the cardiologist's office talking about you critically.

"Mrs. Schmidt is coming in today," one says.

"Oh, she's the one with the difficult daughter," the other replies.

You feel embarrassed and stung and wonder if you've done something to deserve that epithet.

The Solution:

Men are more likely to defend themselves when attacked by disparaging the source of the criticism. They'll say, "Well, what the hell do they know?" Women are more likely to blame themselves and to take criticism as valid without examining it first.

Try to assess on your own if you have been behaving inappropriately. Since you may not be objective, you'll need to get input from other sources. If you have friends working in health care, share with them examples of questions you've been posing and ask if they're within the bounds of acceptable behavior.

If you determine your behavior is appropriate but perhaps unusual, you may also want to talk to the physician directly to clarify your intent and expectations. You can say, for example, "I know I've been asking a lot of questions. I'd like to talk to you about my role in my mother's care."

It's a good bet he'll back off at this point, commenting, "I always welcome an informed consumer."

But if he responds paternalistically, asking, "How about if I be the doctor and you be the daughter?" you might want to consider whether you've got the right cardiologist.

Rule: Evaluate the source of the criticism.

---

5. The Situation:
You want to make partner and you want to make sure you take the appropriate steps.

You're an attorney in a large firm. You feel that you have been quite successful compared with peers who were hired at the same time that you were. The partners give you positive feedback about your work, an unusual occurrence for this firm. Still, you're concerned. You've noticed a clear trend in the organization: Women don't make partner. This is particularly true if they, like you, have taken maternity leave for three months and then become part-timers for several more months before resuming a full schedule.

You want to make all the right moves to become partner. What should you do?

The Solution:

You're right to be concerned if you perceive a trend in your firm away from promoting women to partner. The stated policy often does not reflect reality. Take the following steps to help insure your future success:

1. *Identify those who control your career opportunities.* In your case, that would be the other partners. In other businesses, those individuals might be your boss or others not directly above you but who nevertheless wield great influence in the organization.

2. *Create opportunities to get feedback on how these individuals rate your performance and general contributions to the organization.* These opportunities may be formal (make an appointment) or informal (during a working session).

3. *Ask for feedback.* You might say, "Randy, it was great working on this case with you. I've learned a lot. I'd appreciate any feedback you may have for me regarding how I did and where I can improve."

If your superior answers vaguely, saying, "You're doing just fine," be aware that this is inadequate for your needs. You've got to tease out the negative feedback. You might counter, "Nobody's perfect. What's one thing I could do better?"

4. *Take the criticism seriously.* Be sure to modify your behavior and get follow-up feedback on how those modifications are going.

If the problem is a perception that you're not fully committed to the organization because you have taken maternity leave, you might say, "What can I do now to demonstrate my commitment to the organization?"

Bear in mind, however, that men often withhold negative feedback from women because they fear women will cry. So you must seek out negative feedback in a way that a man might not have to.

Rule: Seek criticism from appropriate sources and tease it out of reluctant informants.

---

6. The Situation:
You know you're going to cry.

You have coordinated the Total Quality Management (TQM) activities in your organization, and you're quite proud of the progress the company has made. Word has gotten out among your peers in the field, and now you've been asked to speak at a national TQM symposium, sharing the work you have done with a broader audience. You're thrilled.

Your organization typically pays for employees at your level to attend one and sometimes two professional meetings a year. And so with great pride, you tell Gene, your boss, about the invitation. Unmoved by your enthusiasm, he says bluntly, "I don't want to waste money on conferences like that."

You're taken aback and feel stung by Gene's comment. You leave the office red-faced without coming to your own defense.

After giving it some thought, however, you feel that you want to broach the subject again with Gene. You believe that maybe he didn't understand the significance of the national conference and the visibility it will give the organization and you. But because you're so attached to and proud of your work and hurt by Gene's previous comment, you feel sure you'll cry during the meeting with him.

You wonder what you can do to prevent or deal with the tears.

The Solution:

Boys grow up being repeatedly told, "Big boys don't cry." Indeed, they learn how to physiologically control the crying mechanism. As we all know, little girls aren't raised with this restriction.

A woman's tendency to cry also has a biological base. One is more likely to cry if the hormone prolactin circulates in one's body. After puberty, females have more of this substance and therefore are more chemically predisposed to crying than are males.

Since men are relatively inexperienced with crying, they're unsure how to handle it. As a result, when someone cries, men try to end the interaction or quickly truncate it.

You have several options for handling the experience of crying.

1. *Get in touch with your true emotions.* Tears are often precipitated by anger held inside. If you go into Gene's office and try to act as if nothing of great import has happened without letting him know how angry you are, there's a good chance you'll cry. Express your anger/disappointment/surprise appropriately by saying, "Gene, I need to let you know how surprised and upset I was when you turned down my request the other day to attend the TQM conference, considering how much work I have put into this project for you." This may seem inappropriate to you, but bear in mind that men often express their emotions through anger. Your anger will probably look more "normal" to Gene.

2. *Pay attention to your breathing.* Just before you start to cry, you may take short, shallow, rapid breaths. This prepares the body for crying. If you slow and deepen your breathing (inhaling as you count to six and exhaling as you count to six), you circumvent the body's mechanism for crying.

3. *Inflict pain on your body.* Some women will dig their fingernails into their wrist or bite their tongue when they feel they're about to cry. Although this strategy sounds masochistic, it does work. When you focus on the physical pain rather than the emotional pain, you distract yourself from crying.

4. *Announce the possibility that you might cry.* Holding the tension in often precipitates the weeping, so if you advertise the cry, the urge may dissipate. (The same is true when you're about to sneeze. If someone asks you if you're going to, you almost never do it.) Therefore, you might say when you go in to meet with your boss, "Gene, I need to talk to you about the TQM conference. I want to let you know that I care a great deal about what I'm going to say to you and because I care so much, I may cry. If I do, it's not a big deal. See, I've brought my own Kleenex." While Gene will probably be surprised by such a statement, at least you're likely to remain dry-eyed.

Rule: Develop strategies for crying.

---

7. The Situation:
Your boss praises you.

As human resources manager, you're responsible for rolling out a new compensation package for your company. You plan the employee presentations and workshops, hold special office hours for those who have questions, establish a hotline, and produce a glossy, comprehensive question-and-answer brochure.

Ed, your boss, calls you into his office and declares, "You know, in the past, every time we changed the compensation package, employees have screamed bloody murder. I've been bracing myself, but this time the silence of my phone has been deafening. It's great! What did you do?"

You're about to say, "Aw, it was nothing. Everyone else helped. I guess I just lucked out." But then you stop and wonder if that's the best approach.

The Solution:

Men have an easier time accepting praise than women do. When men are asked why they did particularly well at a task, they tend to attribute the success to themselves ("Well, you asked me to do it, didn't you?"). When they fail, they tend to attribute the fiasco to factors outside themselves ("You didn't give me enough time").

Conversely, when women succeed, they often don't take credit for it as a man might. They ascribe the success to outside factors such as effort ("I tried real hard"), task ease ("It was easy to begin with"), or luck ("I guess I got lucky on this one"). Unfortunately, when women fail, they usually attribute their defeat to themselves ("I tried but I just couldn't do it").

Moreover, women play down the praise they receive to equalize their status in the hierarchy relative to others. Men feel comfortable having been told that they are higher up on the hierarchy since one of their goals is to be better than others. (Being "better" than someone doesn't affect men's relationships the same way it does women's.)

Instead of discounting the praise that Ed is handing out, accept and extend it by saying, "I appreciate your noticing how much work I put into this project. I was pleased too with how smoothly the transition went. Thanks."

Rule: Accept praise and extend it, if you're comfortable.

8. The Situation:
You don't get praise from your boss.

For the past month you have been slaving over a report that analyzed three strategic options regarding the future of some of your specialty stores. Last week you completed the report and put it on your boss's desk like your first-born child. You've been waiting for Harriet to tell you how wonderful you are, but you've only heard secondhand that she is pleased with your work. You'd really like her to pat you on the back for this job. So you ask Harriet for some feedback, and she replies, "Your report was just fine."

You'd like a heftier pat. Do you work harder at soliciting positive feedback from Harriet?

The Solution:

Boys don't expect praise as much as girls do. They have outside, objective measures of success; all they need do is check the score to know if they have won the game. Girls feel good about their success when others tell them that they've done well. After all, no one keeps score in a game of dolls.

Women feel good about their work and their professional role in general when they get positive feedback. If the praise is absent, a woman begins to feel as if she's not doing a particularly effective job.

You may want and even relish positive feedback from your boss, but in reality some managers just don't give it. If you push, you may look like a dependent weakling.

If Harriet withholds praise, build a support system elsewhere. Get together with other peers to share information about what you're working on. Give each other the accolades you all need to keep on going and doing a great job.

Rule: Exchange praise with peers.

9

Getting to the Goal Line

•••

B oys grow up always focusing on the goal line—that's the purpose of playing the game. They may make a mess and break a lot of rules, but they get the job done. As a result, men are more likely to look at their long-term professional goals early on, and do what they must to meet them.

Women often get caught in believing that every step has to be done correctly without angering anyone or breaking any rules. They are good at performing perfectly, making sure to dot all their i's and cross all their t's. They focus on the process rather than the goal. Consequently, women are apt to wake up one day and wonder about their career direction. They suddenly ask themselves, "What is all my hard work going to get me in the end?"

It's important to formulate a career goal—make partner, become a vice president, outsell the competition—and then define the steps you'll need to take to reach that goal. But don't let yourself become distracted or stymied in your progress to the point that you abandon the goal. The sad truth is, women feel so responsible for the welfare of others that they're often derailed from their goals by meeting others' needs. You've got to decide where to draw the line (even if it means making a mess or leaving some details undone) so that you can get to your personal goal line. The situations and solutions in this chapter will help you define and reach your goals.

1. The Situation:
You've got big aspirations.

You are a nursing supervisor and derive particular enjoyment from patient advocacy, that is, making sure that the patient's needs are not lost in the health care system. You find that you're constantly getting flak from the doctors with whom you work. You know you could have a greater impact on more patients if you were a lawyer, shaping laws and fighting in the courts for patients' rights.

Yet law school seems like an impossible dream. You're married, you have a mortgage, and you and your husband are hoping to start a family in the near future. Should you give up on your dream? And if not, how will you go from being a nurse in this hospital to having a law degree?

The Solution:

You can do anything you want if you decide to. Write down your goal to get a law degree and describe as clearly as you can what you would be doing as a patient advocate. When people do this, they're better able to focus on their objectives; they become more aware of opportunities in their environment and take advantage of them. Written goals become part of everyday life. On the other hand, when goals are left unwritten, other immediately pressing issues in one's life intervene and take precedence. After you've written your goal, post it on the refrigerator door or wherever you will see it daily.

Your goal may seem unattainable and overwhelming because of its immensity, so break it down into smaller parts. Each can become an attainable goal in its own. Decide the first steps you would have to take to reach your goal. These may be:

- calling three law schools in your city to ask for catalogs and financial aid information.

- getting the names of three lawyers who do patient advocacy work and make appointments with them.

- finding out when and where the LSAT preparation courses are being held.

The law degree may seem to be a mountain too large to climb, but these three first steps are quite doable. After you've achieved these, come up with your next three steps until you find yourself in the courtroom.

**Rule: Write down your goals and put them in a visible place.
Break your goals into attainable steps.**

---

2. The Situation:
You demand perfection of yourself.

You're an engineer. Several months ago you received a great compliment from Byron, the president of your company, "You're one of the most forward-thinking individuals in our organization and maybe even in this field. I want you to reevaluate how and where we process our chemicals. Start with a clean slate. Look at our plants in the U.S., Mexico, and Puerto Rico. What should be processed where? Don't feel confined just because we don't have a facility in a particular locale or because we've always done things a certain way. I want you to have free rein in rethinking the organization."

This is your dream assignment. You dive into the work and read as much as you can in the subject area. But every time you read an article, it references others you should study, and those reference even more. Your stack of material to be read is sky-high now. You talk to other individuals about what they do in their organizations and they've all suggested additional people whom you should contact. For three months now, you have been drifting in this ocean of information and feel as if you'll never get it all under your belt.

You hear that Byron is disappointed in you. You've taken too long to come up with a solution. He thinks he may have chosen the wrong individual because he hasn't seen any product yet. How do you help yourself out of this situation?

The Solution:

Perfectionism can result in your never reaching your goals. When you fear that you won't get the job done right, you may procrastinate making tough decisions, or you may become reluctant to take necessary risks to reach your goals. Furthermore, you may try to do it all, believing that no one can do as good a job as you. All of these strategies lead to feeling paralyzed.

The best approach is to look at a task not as an all-or-nothing, I'd-better-get-it-right-on-the-first-pass-or-not-do-it-at-all sort of job, but as a series of successive approximations. Each time you attack your project, you get closer to your goal, until you eventually reach it.

Give yourself a deadline, such as having the first draft in to Byron (and mark it "first draft") by the end of next week. Realize that risk taking is part of success and that you have to allow yourself imperfection if you're going to win at this plum job.

When you see the flaws in your first draft, don't beat yourself up, but make notes about what you've learned. Then use those notes as your springboard to doing the second and maybe even the third draft. (See chapter 8 on self-talk and learning from criticism.)

Rule: Don't demand perfection of yourself.

---

3. The Situation:
You're overwhelmed by your responsibilities.

The following may be your typical schedule:

* You got home late from work last night because you had to finish a report before you left.

* Your daughter reminded you that she promised to bring cookies to a party at school tomorrow, so you stayed up till midnight baking.

* This morning the toilet overflowed and you had to call the plumber and arrange to be home in the afternoon to let him in.

* A family friend is having a birthday party and you need to get him a present.

* A new consultant is wandering around at work. You think she may have an impact on your department so you need to get to know her.

* When you left the house this morning, you noticed that the flowers around your front door were all dead, and you remember that your mother-in-law is visiting this weekend.

How can you manage all of these tasks?

The Solution:

Women are terribly responsible people. When you hear the phrase, "If I don't do it, who will?" it probably came out of the mouth of a woman. Girls are brought up to feel responsible for the physical and psychological well-being of everyone around them. Women don't decide to be responsible; they just take on the burden unconsciously and then feel overwhelmed by all the important items as well as the minutiae.

Despite this, however, you can get your life in order. Here's how:

1. *Decide what's really important.* It's swell if your daughter brings homemade cookies to school, but store-bought goodies will probably suffice for her classmates, who probably love Oreos anyway. On the other hand, meeting with the new consultant at work could have a long-term impact on your department and so should be considered a top priority.

2. *Decide on what might be appropriate to delegate to other individuals.* Your husband might be better able to return from work to wait for the plumber. And, since it is his friend who is having the birthday, it might be more appropriate for your husband to pick up the present.

3. Let go. Certain chores may not be worth your time and effort at this moment. You will all survive if the garden isn't replanted for Mom. You've all got more important things on your mind.

Rule: Consciously decide what your responsibilities are; delegate what's not your responsibility.

---

4. The Situation:
Others don't do the job well enough.

You're proud of the fact that the other night you and your husband had a talk about dividing up responsibilities. You feel good about the outcome because you believe you'll be less overwhelmed and able to focus on what's important. He agreed to buy and mail a birthday present to your father, as well as take on the responsibility of doing the family laundry and some other household chores.

At breakfast, you ask your husband, "What did you buy for my dad, dear?" It's obvious from his blank stare that he forgot. You're mortified. Soon your daughter comes down dressed for school, wearing her lovely white top that is now blotchy pink—the same shade all of your underwear has turned.

You feel the urge to yell at your husband for his lack of attention. In fact, you want to bar him from ever using that washing machine again. You pause and think what to say.

The Solution:

Because women feel so responsible in business and in their personal lives, they will often repossess already delegated tasks if others do them imperfectly. Unfortunately, such behavior adds to one's feelings of being overwhelmed. Perhaps more harmfully, it keeps women from focusing on what's strategically important for them; they stay buried in the details.

When you give up the responsibility, you must also give up the guilt (for not having accomplished a task perfectly and disappointing someone) and butt out. If you feel mortified because your husband has failed to send the birthday present, you must stifle the emotion and let go. Rather, when your mate admits to his mistake, you might ask cheerily, "Were you planning to send it this week?"

When your daughter comes down wearing her newly "pink" top, you might joke, "That's an interesting shade of pink. I didn't think I'd ever seen that color until this morning, when I put on my underwear. Do you want to see?"

But however you respond, do not take back these responsibilities. They're not yours anymore.

Rule: Don't reassume responsibilities you've delegated.

---

5. The Situation:
You've run into a lot of roadblocks.

The divisional director has given you an exciting and challenging assignment: creating a discount retail outlet for the clothing your company manufactures. Barbara wants it up and running in four weeks.

As you start to organize the project, you find yourself encountering a lot of difficulties:

+ Human resources told you that you have to post the job openings for four weeks before you can even hire anybody.

+ Facilities says you can't move into the designated area until the bathrooms have been remodeled for handicapped access.

+ Purchasing says they will have to process your computer requisition, and that will take two months.

+ Renee, the person in charge of the phone system, is on vacation for three weeks, and you're told she has to approve all installations.

You go back to Barbara and tell her, "I tried, but I can't have the retail outlet running in the time that you want." You then go on to explain all the obstacles.

Rather than relenting or sympathizing, Barbara gets angry. She says, "Look, Linda, if you can't get the job done, I'll just give it to someone else."

What might have been a better strategy?

The Solution:

Executives don't want to hear why things can't be done; they only want to hear when a task has been accomplished. Your job is to figure out how to pull off this assignment. Given all the obstacles, you're going to have to figure out how you'll get around them in order to do the job. For instance:

+ You might consider hiring temporary help to staff the store before interviewing official applicants.

+ You might move into the area first and remodel the bathrooms later.

+ You might borrow another department's excess computers or just go out and buy them without the purchasing department's blessing—just let your boss know in advance.

- You might go directly to the phone service provider to set up the system. When Renee comes back from vacation, she might be angry and feel that you've usurped her power, but the real issue is that you opened the store on time. Barbara is your boss; she, not Renee, impacts your career.

Rule: Be stubborn about achieving your goals, even if it means bending some rules.

---

6. The Situation:
You're late turning in an important project.

You're the director of clinical services for a nonprofit health care agency. Jackie, the executive director, has asked you to prepare a training manual for your staff. You've made progress on it but haven't been able to finish on deadline. First, you can't find the time to go down to the printer to choose the graphics and paper stock. You also want to write out a policy statement about the manual's distribution. You'd like to fine-tune the writing for part of it. The phones haven't stopped ringing.

Jackie has pressured you to finish the job, and you have told her that you will get it done as soon as possible, but you fear that she will take this project away from you if you don't complete it soon. What should you do?

The Solution:

This project is really important to your boss, so you need to finish it. Identify the issues critical to Jackie, and resolve those. That may mean letting go of some of the details: The graphics may not be exactly what you had envisioned, or maybe the printer will have to choose the paper stock. Have someone else answer the phones and return your calls. And since it's most important to Jackie to have the manual in hand, finish it first and worry about the distribution policy later.

Rule: Don't get caught in the details; focus on the larger goal.

---

7. The Situation:
You never seem to be able to get your work done.

Here is a typical day at the office:

- ◆ Carl is having a problem with the new project and needs to talk to you about it.
- ◆ Francine is arguing with Cheryl because Cheryl doesn't help her as much as Francine believes she should.
- ◆ Lydia comes in with red eyes and tells you that she and her husband are on the verge of divorce. She admits that it's hard for her to concentrate. She came to apologize for the poor quality of her work, but ends up telling you the whole saga of the marriage.
- ◆ Steve stops by to show you his vacation pictures.
- ◆ Tim has a great idea for eliminating the glitches you've been experiencing with your new computer system.
- ◆ Chris wants to update you on a report she has been working on.

It's now five o'clock, and you're still looking at the same mound of paper that was on your desk when you walked in this morning. You'll probably be here till late in the evening, finishing the work you had hoped you would get done today. (On other days such as this, you go home with a sense of panic.) Is there a better way to handle your time and workload?

The Solution:

Studies have shown that in organizations women are twice as available as men. Picture this: The man is in his office, door closed, getting his work done. The woman is in her office, door opened, meeting everyone else's needs but her own. At the end of his day, he's ready to go home; at the end of her day, she's ready to start on her own agenda.

Limit your availability. You may want to consider keeping your door closed part of the day to signal that you're not constantly accessible to whoever wants to stop by. If you're working on a pressure-filled, time-limited project and are interrupted by someone with less than critical concerns, you might say, "I need to get this finished. Could we talk after lunch?"

Of course, there may be times when you must stop what you're doing to meet others' needs. The key is to get strategic about making these decisions and stop yourself from automatically shifting into the Earth Mother role.

Rule: Strategically limit your availability.

8. The Situation:
You're in an unsupportive environment.

In your last job, you worked for a small consulting firm where the culture was friendly and supportive. Now you've made a significant career move into a large, prestigious firm. However, after a few weeks on the job, it has become clear to you that only a few employees become vice presidents. As a result, the culture of this organization is highly competitive. Your co-workers are sharks, and you don't know who you can trust or which moves will be to your advantage.

You start to feel unhappy about your new job. It's a lonely place to work. You miss the old crowd but you know you can't go back there. How can you help yourself in this new situation?

The Solution:

It would be wonderful if you had a boss whom you trusted and who would guide you, and co-workers on whom you could depend. But that isn't the case in your situation. It's clear that you're not going to find your support system at work.

To be successful, you have to have a support system behind you. Relationships are critical to your professional success as well as to your personal well-being. Look for support external to the organization. Join industry-specific organizations as well as more general networking groups such as Women in Business. Also, set up an informal network of friends and colleagues with whom you can lunch and talk about career strategies and opportunities. Don't forget that your family and personal friends are an important part of your support system. (Also see chapter 11, situation #2 on choosing an appropriate corporate culture.)

Rule: Create a personal and professional support system.

---

9. The Situation:
The "big shots" want time you do not have.

You work in the airline industry. Specifically, your department interfaces with the Federal Aviation Administration in regulation compliance. Like many of your competitors in the industry, your company has been laying off employees, and your department has lost several positions. As a result, you've had more work to do with fewer people. You feel as if you're running on empty lately, trying to get everything done.

Your boss tells you that the chief operating officer has requested that you join a new 14-member committee being established to assess how to restructure the organization to run more effectively. You've barely been able to get things done as it is; this new assignment, though prestigious, would take another big chunk of your time. You could not possibly do well at your present job and work on this committee. Do you agree to join the committee?

The Solution:

Sometimes we get so preoccupied with what is making immediate demands on our time that we can't see the larger picture. In this case, you may be unaware of how this extra work for a "big shot" might contribute greatly to future advancement.

Thank your boss for the opportunity to work on this committee and graciously accept, even if your heart goes into palpitations because you can't figure out how you're going to pull it off.

If your goal is to climb the corporate ladder in this organization, you must look at your career-move choices strategically. It can seem to you that your most important task is the completion of your day-to-day work, but what will really impact your career dramatically in the long term is this high-visibility position on the committee. In fact, if some of your other work falls through the cracks as a result of your time spent on the restructuring committee, that probably won't dramatically impact your future opportunities as much as your declining this invitation would.

Rule: Make yourself available to the powers-that-be.

$$\diamond\ 10\ \diamond$$

Winning the Game

◆◆◆

W omen come into the workplace with the per-
spective that fairness will prevail. If you do the
best job ever, and if you do it faster and cheaper,
you will be rewarded accordingly. Unfortunately, Hardball
isn't played that way.

When women sit nose to the grindstone, doing a good
job, men perceive them as being impotent and easily
duped. They're certainly not someone to contend with.

Politics, strategy, and who you know often drive one's
success. It isn't right, it isn't fair, but it's just the way it is. If
you want to be successful, you have to know how the game
is played. You have to take risks, make your accomplishments known, fight to be paid well, and realize that social
events are in fact political opportunities. You have to take
charge of your career in order to advance and win at the
game. This chapter will show you how.

1. The Situation:
You've got great evaluations but little else.

You work in an accounting firm, and you're hoping for a big promotion someday. Your seniors have told you that you're one of the best managers in the firm. Clearly, others like to work for you and as a result they are more productive when they're part of your team. You'd love the opportunity to move up. Yet it seems that in this organization, who you know, who you lunch with, who you golf with has a lot to do with promotions. Since you hope to move up, you're wondering if your great evaluations will do you any good.

The Solution:

You're right: The people getting promoted are probably those who are the heavy-duty networkers rather than the managers with the most productive and committed employees. Research has found that highly effective managers (those whose employees are exceptionally committed to the organization and the department and extremely productive both in quality and quantity of work) often are not the managers who move up. Instead, those who network (41 percent of their time on average) with people throughout the organization are more likely to get the best positions.

Identify the movers and shakers in your firm and begin to network with them, whether you just stop by their office to say hi and drop off some documents, or ask them out to lunch, or even learn how to play golf.

Don't sacrifice being a good manager for networking, but mentally add networking to your job description.

Rule: Network, network, network.

---

2. The Situation:
You don't want to go to the company party.

It is December 15 and you're dog-tired. You're an escrow officer at a bank, and for tax reasons many of your deals are closing before the first of the year. You've spent the last weeks buying Christmas presents, baking gingerbread for the kids' parties at school, decorating the house, and sending holiday cards. This Friday is the company Christmas party and all you want to do is go home and pass out. You figure nobody will miss you. Should you attend or stay home to relax with your family?

The Solution:

Women often think that social functions are only for social purposes. They fail to understand that these gatherings are really about networking, making contacts, building relationships for future needs, demonstrating commitment to the company, making informal assessments for potential jobs, building trust, and so on.

When you receive the announcement of the Christmas bash, consider it an opportunity to help you solve future problems, position yourself for advancement, and get what you need. Also realize that your absence will send as much a message to the power brokers as will your presence. They may read your absence as a lack of commitment to the organization or team.

Grin and bear it and see this party as just another part of your job. When you have to get a report in by Thursday, you do it whether you want to or not. Likewise, when a company party is announced, you must attend whether you want to or not.

Rule: Attend company social functions even if you don't want to.

---

3. The Situation:
You're not getting ahead as fast as you'd like.

You work in a lab in the R&D department of a large telecommunications company. You're a hard worker: You're productive and you receive good performance appraisals. Arthur, your boss, tells you frequently that he is pleased with your output. You're happy with the praise but feel it would be inappropriate to draw any attention to it. You always figured that if you did a good job, you'd be rewarded for it.

So why are you stuck in your current position?

The Solution:

Boys grow up talking about their successes in the game last weekend. As a result, it is often much easier for men to bring the conversation around to their accomplishments. But good girls don't brag. In fact, when attention is drawn to a woman's success, she will often divert the conversation from herself.

Furthermore, women are really good at working hard, but nobody is aware of their accomplishments because it would be unladylike for a woman to talk about or otherwise draw attention to herself. In reality, however, people are promoted based on what's known about them. Moreover, women are often perceived as being pleased with their present positions. Senior individuals often don't have a clue that they want to move up.

Start tooting your own horn. No one else is going to do it for you. Arthur may be pleased with your work, but does he tell anybody else? Does he know that you want to advance in the company? Identify your skills and accomplishments, figure out who needs to know about them, and then practice talking about yourself, maybe with a good friend or trusted colleague who would give you feedback. Then, whenever the opportunity arises, do what men do: Gradually include information about your successes.

In addition, whenever you get positive feedback from Arthur or others, ask them to communicate it verbally or, better yet, in writing to the power brokers with whom they are connected.

Rule: Make your accomplishments and goals known.
Be sure the power brokers know who you are
and what you've done.

---

4. The Situation:
You're asked to take a big risk.

You are a production supervisor in a new division of an automotive firm. Your division has innovated effective manufacturing procedures. Some leaders in the automotive field have recommended that some-one from your division speak at an upcoming national conference. Sam, your boss, has asked you to deliver the address.

More than a thousand people will be present at the conference, and your hands are already beginning to sweat. Rarely do you speak to groups, and you've never spoken to more than 50 people at one time. You can't imagine making this national address, and you're about to ask Sam to find someone else when a little voice in your head says, "Should I or shouldn't I?"

The Solution:

Boys learn that the only way to win the big game is to take risks. Girls are discouraged from taking risks and in fact are admonished against them. "Get out of that tree," we are told. "You're going to hurt yourself." Consequently, women will often turn away from professional risks.

But Sam has offered you a wonderful opportunity to learn about risk taking. Take a deep breath and thank him for inviting you to make the address. Tell him you'd be glad to. Recognize that you won't do this perfectly and that you're going to need to acquire some skills to prepare you for the speech. For example, you may wish to take a course in public speaking. Maybe you can arrange to give this same speech within the company or to a professional organization before the big conference. Be sure to take the opportunity to enhance your visibility within and outside your organization.

Rule: Take calculated professional risks.

---

5. The Situation:
You feel sleazy about pushing for more money.

You are outside your boss's office and need to make a phone call. Cynthia, your boss, invites you in and says, "Go ahead, use my phone."

As you sit down at her desk, you notice that the department's budget package is lying open to the salary scale page. Not one to look away, you quickly peruse the list. Much to your amazement, you discover that Matt, a co-worker who has been at the company as long as you have, with the same educational background and experience, is making thousands more per year than you are. You're not angry at him, but you are bent out of shape that you're paid less. You want to talk to Cynthia about it but you don't know if you should. You don't want to seem money hungry.

The Solution:

In the male culture, money is related to status and success. Because men associate money so strongly with their worth as people, they're willing to fight for more. Because women are motivated by internal rewards like pride in work or sense of accomplishment, they're less likely to push for money. They're also less apt to demand it in order to avoid appearing too ambitious or money hungry.

Initially, it's wise to solve the problem without mentioning that you've seen the pay scale. If it's close to the time that salary increases come out, wait until then before bringing up the subject. If salary review is more than six months away, however, make an appointment to talk with Cynthia about your concerns.

When you meet with her, be prepared to negotiate your increase. (See the strategies in situation #6 below.) If your negotiations for an increase do not result in equitable pay, then mention Matt's salary and ask Cynthia for help in understanding what skills or education you need to be paid as much as he is. This signals to her that you know the disparity without putting her on the defensive.

Rule: Stick up for your right to be paid well.

6. The Situation:
You don't know how to get a raise.

You work in the real estate division of a retail clothing chain. Your primary responsibility has been to negotiate contracts with malls for your stores. Your boss has quit to take a job with a competing company and you have been offered his managerial position.

You're very honored and excited about what you can accomplish, but you're also a bit anxious. Your new job will require you to travel, and you're concerned about child care arrangements for your five-year-old daughter. Next week you're going to be sitting down with Richard, who will be your new boss, to talk about your job as well as your pay. What should you do to prepare for the salary negotiation?

The Solution:

Women often feel so personally honored by promotion opportunities that negotiating a salary seems rather pushy to them. Consequently, they don't do their homework when it comes to salary negotiation and are grateful for whatever they get in the way of an increase. Many believe that whatever dollar amount they're told is fixed in concrete rather than negotiable.

Accept the fact that you deserve more money for doing a bigger job. Keep in mind that organizations will often pay you as little as possible. If you don't ask for more, you won't get more. So use the following strategies to help you get a raise:

1. *Conduct objective research on how much money your position earns.* Investigate how much other people who hold this type of position in a company the size of yours and in a similar geographic area are paid. Professional organizations frequently do salary surveys and are most helpful in this regard. Ideally, find out how much your previous boss had been paid.

2. *Document what you have contributed financially to the organization.* Estimate how much money you have saved or made for the company in the past years. For instance, have you been able to secure a lower rent when renegotiating contracts? If you can, put a dollar number next to your contribution to the company.

3. *Ask for the pay you deserve, not what you need.* You may feel that you need more money to pay for your child's baby-sitter while you're traveling, but this is of no concern to your boss. It's better to simply ask for what you deserve rather than what you believe you need. If you get what you deserve, you'll cover your needs anyway.

4. *Be aware that the salary point system is subjective.* Most large organizations have a point system to determine salaries. The points establish one's salary range. Be wary of these. For instance, you may be told that you have 33 points, as if it is a fact that prevents you from getting a higher salary. Keep in mind that somebody sat down and subjectively decided how many points you have. This same individual can subjectively redetermine that you have more points if the powers-that-be decide you do.

Rule: Do your homework in salary negotiations.

---

7. The Situation:
You're confused by the company's mission statement.

You're an assistant manager of a large department store. Your company's mission statement says very clearly that the customer comes first. You've taken this to heart and make frequent suggestions about ways that your store and even the entire chain could improve service to the customer. You've recommended, for example, a briefcase checkroom for working women, child care for mothers who want to browse unencumbered, and valet parking.

Your superiors have consistently and quickly dismissed your proposals, so you've decided to pay attention to whose ideas are taken seriously and whether this translates into promotions. After several months of observation, it becomes clear that those who slash costs with little concern for the customer are getting ahead in this organization.

You feel caught in a schizophrenic situation: On the one hand, you're told that the customers are all-important; on the other hand, the people who get promoted actually pay minimal attention to customers. What are you supposed to do?

The Solution:

You're wise to observe who is getting promoted around you. That will tell you what the company really values and therefore what you need to do if you want to move up. Organizations frequently devise mission statements filled with hearts and flowers: "The customer comes first"; "Quality is all that matters." Often this has nothing to do with how the organization really works. In reality promotions are unrelated to the company's published mission.

Put your energy into saving the company money and you're more likely to get ahead.

Rule: Know and play to your company's bottom line; don't get hooked into the party line.

---

8. The Situation:
Your boss doesn't know what she's doing.

You work in a high-tech audio/video department of a company that creates extravagant meetings and parties for large corporations. You've just been assigned a new manager, Allison. You've decided that she must be somebody's friend or relative because she knows very little about cutting-edge audio/video technology.

You're irritated that the powers-that-be have hired someone so incompetent. You find yourself having to educate and fill in for Allison. When she brings you along to meet with clients, you do most of the explaining and answer most of the questions.

You've been thinking about avoiding these meetings so that the higher-ups will realize how incompetent Allison truly is. Indeed, she came to you the other day and asked your opinion about the best equipment to use for videotaping a complicated presentation. You replied, "I really don't know," even though you did. And you had a sense that Allison knew you were trying to pull the wool over her eyes.

You're not sure if you should sit back and watch Allison go down in flames or do her job for her.

The Solution:

In organizations, the boss frequently does not know how to do the employees' jobs. This becomes more common as one moves up in the hierarchy. (The president of the company certainly doesn't know how to do all the jobs within the company.)

A successful employee is one who will make the boss look good. This is especially true because the boss can make or break the employee's career. You may not like it; it may feel unfair to you, especially if you feel that your boss is incompetent, but no matter what, she's your boss. She has the power. In large part, she determines your success.

If Allison knows that you can and will help her, you'll earn points with her that will probably result in future career opportunities for you. If she knows that you can help but won't, however, she's likely to feel sabotaged and then will return the favor, undercutting your career.

The best thing you can do is get on her side and take advantage of what she can do for you.

Rule: Make the boss look good.

Your Game Plan

♦♦♦

I n discussing game plans, I like to mention the boiled frog syndrome. If you put a frog in boiling water, it'll jump right out. But if you place it in a pot of cold water that you slowly heat to boiling, the frog will stay inside and boil to death. There is no single point at which the water becomes too hot and lets the frog know it's time to extricate itself from a bad situation.

Unfortunately, the same can often be said of employees. They may be working in an environment that is uncomfortable, unrewarding, or unchallenging or for a boss who can't see their strengths. Or, they may be in an industry or position that doesn't provide growth or job security. Still, they stay there for years, complaining and hoping that their lot will improve but knowing that it really won't. There's no point at which the water becomes so hot that they realize they must move on. They just sit and stew in their unhappiness.

There is a solution to the boiled frog syndrome, but it requires strength and courage. People do make changes in their lives once they realize how unhappy they are. But they need to know when it's time to move on and how to go about it.

Scan your environment to decide if you're getting the payoffs that you want. If you're not, this chapter provides strategies for getting you out of hot water before it's too late.

1. The Situation:
You're unsure of your next career move.

As the manager in the security department of a midsize city, you plan security systems for new and remodeled municipal facilities. You've enjoyed your job for the past 10 years, but you're beginning to wonder where you're going. You've noticed that your upward momentum in the organization has slowed considerably. Indeed, you're skeptical about your chances for advancement, since there are no other women at your level or above in the security area.

For the third time, one of your male peers has been selected to move up. From everything you can assess, your performance has been better than all three men who were promoted before you. You're questioning your long-term career goals and wonder if you'll ever advance in this old-boy system.

The Solution:

It's time for you to take a hard look at your professional direction. Do you want to continue to move up the management ladder and acquire the increased responsibilities and perks that go along with an executive position? Do you enjoy your professional work so much that you would prefer to stay in a more technical position and become well known for your expertise?

Once you've decided on your goal line, consider alternative moves that can get you there. For instance, if you feel you'll never overcome the old-boy network in your department, an internal move to another department with the city might be appropriate. If you want to move up into a larger pond where you can become a bigger fish, relocating to a larger city might be the answer. Keep in mind that, given your profession, you'll probably find the old-boy network there, too.

If you believe you'll never win the battles in your organization, or if you are tired of fighting the antifemale bias, you might choose to go out on your own and start your own company.

The key here is to delineate your long-term career goals. Act on that decision, particularly if you are unhappy in your current situation. It probably won't get better tomorrow. Don't wallow in your pain. Pick yourself up and do something about it.

**Rule: Devise a game plan for your career.
Assess whether you're satisfied in your current position;
stay if you are, plan if you're not.**

---

2. The Situation:
You find yourself in a "party-hearty" company.

You are the regional sales manager for a large dairy and cheese corporation. Initially you thought this was a great organization because everyone was so friendly and outgoing. The employees frequently talked about the parties the company threw and seemed to have great fun together.

Now that you've been with this organization for six months, however, it has become clear to you that these parties are more than potlucks with the family. Employees regularly go out drinking together during the week and expect you to accompany the gang on Friday nights. The company frequently throws employees-only parties. This didn't seem suspicious to you at first, because you've been to many business functions without spouses, but now that you've attended a few, you realize that these bashes are an opportunity for people to get drunk; some even have sexual relations.

This isn't your cup of tea. You're happily married and would rather go home at the end of the day. You have no intention of having an affair. But now others are teasing you about being a stick in the mud. They say, "C'mon, loosen up." And you're being called the "li'l ol' schoolmarm." What should you do?

The Solution:

All organizations have a corporate culture. These cultures can be widely disparate. Companies can be cutthroat, caring, work-till-you-drop, intellectual, seat-of-the-pants, by-the-book, conservative, or "party hearty." And you, much to your dismay, have found yourself in a party-hearty organization. It's easy to see how you were fooled; initially, this kind of company can seem like a friendly environment.

In shopping for a job, just as you need to make certain you fit the requirements, you should also ascertain if the corporate culture suits your temperament and lifestyle. To learn about the company's culture seek out other employees and ask such pointed questions as:

- "What do you do in the evenings?" If the response is, "Oh, we're all here till 9 p.m.," this is probably a work-till-you-drop company.
- "Are there any social functions after work or on weekends?" If the response is, "The only time we get together is at the annual company picnic and the Christmas party," this is probably an organization that doesn't socialize much outside work hours.

- "What are your conventions like?" If the response is, "We have a really good time" or "There's lots of partying going on," you need to determine what kind of partying takes place.

You might have to stay with this job because economic circumstances offer few alternatives. Recognize, then, that you may always be on the periphery of the organization. On the other hand, if this is a critical time for your career growth, and you feel you can't move ahead because the company is so out of sync with your values, then it might be wise to seek other employment.

The bottom line: Make sure that your values fit the company's. You can have the greatest job in the world and still feel unsuccessful and unhappy because you don't fit in.

Rule: Recognize your organization's corporate culture. Accept it or move on.

---

3. The Situation:
You've just been laid off.

You work in the display advertising department of a large newspaper. This morning your boss called you in and told you that unfortunately you're one of the unlucky people included in the layoff.

You're shocked and stunned. You think, "This only happens to other people." You don't have a clue about where to begin finding a new job. You were happy in your position and intended to stay there forever.

You clean out your desk and are about to reach for the classifieds to see what else might be available when you stop and wonder whether this is the most effective way to find a job.

The Solution:

Research has clearly shown that the best way to find a job is to pick up the phone, not the newspaper. Networking accounts for 75 percent of all jobs landed.

Figure out your long-term goals (See situation #1 in this chapter). Then make a list of all your contacts. Phone them one at a time. Inform each individual that you're looking for a position. Ask: "Do you know of any opportunities for me?" and/or "Given my background and interests, is there anyone else I should talk to?" Add any suggested names to your list of people to call.

Be diligent about your job search. Think of it as your new, temporary, full-time position.

Rule: Network to locate other job opportunities.

---

4. The Situation:
You're interviewing at a company you're unfamiliar with.

You're a recently laid-off accountant. You've done your networking homework. A colleague of a friend passed along your résumé to the budget department of The James Company. Soon, you get a call from Flo, the financial director. "I received your résumé and am interested in talking to you about a position," she begins. "I don't know if you're familiar with our company. We make pharmaceutical testing equipment and software."

You've never heard of this organization, but you don't want to appear dumb by asking Flo a lot of questions. So you say, "I've heard the name, but I'm not very familiar with the company. Tell me a little about it."

Flo replies, "We're a subsidiary of the Charles Corporation. We've been in business for 10 years and have grown very rapidly in the last two. We're located in the northern suburbs."

Although Flo has been helpful, she doesn't give you nearly enough information for an interview. What do you do?

The Solution:

Job interviews are successful when you are informed about the organization and can tie yourself to the company's values, goals, problems, and opportunities.

If the company is publicly held, you can call their headquarters and ask for an annual report to be sent to you. The report will, of course, inform you of the company's financial status, but it will also give you a good feel for what's important in that organization, its current problems, and its future aspirations.

If the company is privately owned, your research is more difficult but not impossible. Go to the library and search for articles written about the organization or the industry. In fact, you might want to do this even if you're already in possession of an annual report.

Now that you have some background about the organization, do some hard thinking. Come up with probing questions that will inform your interviewer that you're aware of the company's concerns. In evaluating your experience and skills, think about how you can describe them as being of particular value to the company. For instance, if this is a fast-paced organization, you would talk about a computer program you developed that will allow the company to track its financial status on a daily (rather than monthly or quarterly) basis.

Rule: Research the organization before you interview.

5. The Situation:
You can't decide which job to take.

You're in the enviable position of having two new jobs from which to choose. The first is a move to another organization with a significant jump in title to vice president and wonderful opportunities to grow; the company is having all kinds of problems that you know you can solve. It includes a car allowance and a 20-percent pay increase. You would be reporting to Scott, a top executive. But there is a problem here: Something about your prospective boss doesn't feel right to you. You sense that he's smarmy—a potential snake in the grass. You just know that he got to his exalted position by stepping on others.

Your other option is to stay at the company where you are presently employed and move up only one level to assistant director. You'd receive a disappointing 7-percent pay increase, but you'd be working for Dennis, who has a great track record in growing people.

Which do you choose?

The Solution:

Probably one of the most important factors of a job is one's boss. A great boss can make a mediocre job a springboard to success. A poor boss can make the most wonderful opportunity a hell on earth.

In general you'll always be ahead if you choose a great boss, even if the position is unimpressive, than if you choose a glorious title and position but end up reporting to a rat. Great bosses (those who develop people) give their employees opportunities to work in areas that take advantage of their strengths, even if those areas are outside their job description. With Dennis as your manager, your natural strengths will come to the fore, and those in power will have the opportunity to see what you can contribute to the organization.

If you end up reporting to Scott, you may have a harder time of it. Often such bosses are so concerned about anyone challenging their position in the limelight that they denigrate their personnel and keep them in their place. These bosses are jealous and competitive with their employees. Indeed, if an employee begins to look too good, such a boss will find a way to sabotage her.

Rule: Choose a good boss over a good job.

---

6. The Situation:
You're unsure how to negotiate a new salary.

You're interviewing for a job as manager of marketing at a new company. You've been back three times now, and it seems as if Ellen, your prospective boss, is about to offer you the position. You would bet that the next time you go back to meet with her, she's going to talk salary with you. You don't want to be unreasonable in your expectations for remuneration, but you don't want to roll over and play dead either. How should you negotiate your new salary?

The Solution:

It's wise to come into a salary negotiation armed with information so that you can speak from a position of power. Understanding how compensation systems work in most organizations is critical to gauging how much latitude you have in a salary negotiation. Often salaries and salary scales will be presented as black-and-white, take-it-or-leave-it, objectively determined progressions, when in truth they are fluid and amorphous and based on subjective data.

Also, refrain from discussing salary during the first interview. Wait until the prospective boss has brought up the issue. Ideally, as soon as Ellen broaches the subject of salary, ask her about the range for this position. Be sure to do this before she has the opportunity to question you about how much you're making at your old job. She may base her offer on your current take-home, so some strategic planning is necessary.

To calculate how much you make in your old position, combine your present salary, including the dollar amount of benefits; any other perks you might receive including a car allowance; bonuses or stock options; and any salary increases that may be coming in the near future. Keep in mind that it is virtually impossible for Ellen to check on how much you're really making.

If she says, "The range is between $50,000 and $60,000," you might simply say, "Ah, $60,000," to mark that as your point of reference or departure. If you're already making more than that (after having added in all the above items), let her know that by disclosing the amount.

If she comes back with, "Gee, that's out of our range," you might reply, "Why don't we rethink the position. Can we change the job description to reflect what I would be doing for you?" (See the discussion of the slippery point system in chapter 10, situation #6.) If she really wants you, she might be able to work the system to your advantage.

If you're making less than what Ellen is offering you, contain your glee. Just say, "I think that fits what I was looking for." But at no time should you disclose your old salary.

Also, if you're changing geographic locales, keep in mind that there might be a disparity between salaries and cost of living from one region of the country to another. In making that geographic transition, research the going rate for your job by talking to others in the same profession in this new area or by contacting your professional organization.

Rule: Be astute and do some research in negotiating a new salary.

7. The Situation:
You're offered a position with a great title.

You've worked in the engineering department of Smith Air Conditioning for 20 years. You have noticed, particularly in the past five years, that the men hired into this department generally get promoted out, but you haven't. You've moved up very slowly in your tenure with Smith. For the past year and a half, you've been asking a lot of questions such as, "What do I need to do to get promoted around here?"

Albert, your boss, has continuously told you, "You're doing just fine. I'm sure there will be opportunities for you in the future." But these platitudes aren't translating into action.

You have been putting extra pressure on Albert to help you get promoted. He meets with you and says with great enthusiasm, "I've got good news for you. We're promoting you to director of quality. It's the wave of the future."

This is a new position, so you're not sure about the significance of it, but at least it's a move up from the manager level you've been at. And so you respond, "Gee, that's great. What's the budget going to be for this new department?"

"Don't worry about that," he replies. "I'll take care of the budget."

You inquire, "How many employees will I have in this department?"

Albert's reply: "We're really not sure right now."

You're excited but suspicious. Is this a promotion or a come-on?

The Solution:

It may actually be true that this is an important new position that hasn't yet been fully thought through. In this case you might take the lead and say, "Let me outline what I could contribute to the organization as the director of quality and what it would take in terms of budget and other resources. I'll pull together a job description, and then we can talk."

If the powers-that-be sign off on this proposal, you'll know that this is a serious offer and may be a great opportunity for you. If their response is vague and they don't approve a budget, then back off until the position is more solidified.

Such evasive strategies tell you that the organization is trying to pull the old title trick. Often when a woman is making noise about the fact that the men are being promoted and she is not, the chiefs become restless. To sidetrack her from pointing to the inequities in the organization, they will often give her a great title that means nothing.

Because she feels that she received the promotion she has asked for, she becomes uncomfortable complaining about her dwindling opportunities.

But, in truth, by bestowing on her an empty title, the powers-that-be have effectively shut her up. Her assignments are tangential and don't impact the bottom line. No one returns her phone calls, and when she tries to get monies to actually make a difference, her superiors tell her that it's not in the budget.

Titles without resources to back them mean nothing. If the new position is hollow, it won't take long for others in the organization to figure out that you've got an impressive business card but not much more. The questions that you asked about the budget and employees were right on target. If the organization truly wants to move you ahead, they should put their money where their mouth is. If they don't, you're left to assess where you want to go with your career. Is this the right place for you? (See situation #1 in this chapter.)

Rule: Don't fall for the old title trick.

---

8. The Situation:
You want a job with clout.

You've been hired right out of school into an executive trainee position of a hospital corporation. The program is two years long, and you will change jobs every six months. You're allowed to work in almost any area of the business during this period, including the many layers of hospital administration (from individual hospitals to the corporate structure), human resources, marketing, information systems, real estate, and accounting. Which areas do you choose?

The Solution:

Organizations are composed of two types of work: line and staff. The line function is the core of the business. The staff function supports the line. This varies from industry to industry. For example, in a legal firm, being a lawyer is working in a line function. The accountants are staff. In an accounting firm the CPAs are in line positions, while the attorneys are staff.

The value of one's work is always higher if one is in a line position. Staff functions are usually perceived as overhead and are the first to go in a money crunch. You will find a disproportionate number of women in staff positions.

First, you must determine the line function in the organization. In this company it's hospital administration. Focus on working with those who are in line functions (hospital administrators, regional or divisional directors, or the corporate level).

If you're working in a staff function, assess how you can tie your work more closely to the line function. For instance, if you're in information systems and have an opportunity to redesign reports, it would be better to opt for those that go to the hospital rather than those that go to human resources.

But what if you're passionately interested in marketing and think that might be your future? In this case it would still behoove you to get as much line experience as possible. For the rest of your career, the more you can talk the lingo of the line function and understand its problems, the more successful you're going to be, no matter what staff function you choose.

Rule: Opt for the line position.

---

9. The Situation:
Your boss thinks you're dumb.

You made a mistake. You thought that by accepting a position as an administrative assistant in a property management firm, you'd get your foot in the door. As it turns out, now that you've been labeled "secretarial staff," your superiors see you as a bimbo. You've pointed out that you have a college degree and can do more, but no one takes you seriously.

Your boss, Isabelle, is responsible for managing a wide variety of office buildings throughout the state. She has been complaining to you about the new individual reports that she's expected to produce on all of the properties. The current computer system combines the properties by geographic region.

You're familiar with the computer program that's required to create separate reports. You used it in college. You're thinking about offering to change the system to streamline Isabelle's workload. But this isn't your job. Besides, you're not getting paid for it, and you'll have to stay late for several nights to do it. Should you volunteer?

The Solution:

Secretaries, or administrative assistants as they're now called, are the heartbeat of organizations and keep them running smoothly, but women in these positions receive low pay and little respect for their intelligence. It is usually a mistake for a woman to think that she can get a foothold in an organization by entering on the secretarial level and working her way up. That only happens in the movies.

Unfortunately, you're going to have to fight your way out of the box you've inadvertently put yourself in. You'll have to prove to the powers-that-be, including Isabelle, that you have a brain and can do far more than your job description indicates. You're actually going to have to do the computer work without getting paid for it before anyone will believe you can do it. Once you display your abilities, others may see you as capable of taking on more challenging and ultimately more rewarding assignments.

If you offer to devise the computer report and are turned down and put back in your secretarial box, the sad truth is you'll probably have to leave this organization. You've now got a big red S on your chest, and changing companies is the only way to get rid of it.

Rule: Fight your way out of career-limiting stereotypes.

---

10. The Situation:
You want to expand your career options.

You're a chemist in a cosmetics company but you don't want to remain a chemist for the rest of your life. You'd like to move to a more senior position in which you would grow with the company, yet you don't want to return to school for retraining. In addition, you're aware that layoffs are becoming a way of life for many of your colleagues in other organizations. You'd like to protect yourself in the event that you're a victim of a reduction in force (RIF). What can you do to stay employed in the short term and to position yourself for additional opportunities in the long term?

The Solution:

There is a lot of change afoot in the world right now, and no matter what your position today, you can't count on it existing 10 years from now. However, "employability" will prepare you for the future. Employability means having an array of skills that are applicable in a variety of settings. It also means being flexible in how you perceive your job.

Senior executives are individuals who have created opportunities to learn about many areas other than their own. By expanding your knowledge base, you're able to recognize how various functions link together or create problems for one another. Companies in the future will be looking for individuals who are able and eager to work in a number of functions.

The name of the game is skills and knowledge. Your best strategy to prepare for the short and long term is to acquire an assortment of practical knowledge that's transferable to different settings. For example, even though you were hired as a chemist, you can learn more about your company's financial reports or get involved in operations and manufacturing. You can also become knowledgeable about the company's strategic direction and understand the marketing and sales process.

You can achieve these goals by volunteering to be on committees, becoming involved in projects outside the normal scope of your job, and reading and attending in-house seminars that most of your chemist colleagues see as irrelevant.

These strategies not only will make you more valuable and less likely to be laid off when the RIF comes, but will also help set you up for more senior positions in the future. You'll have gained an understanding of the workings of the entire company, not just your narrow field.

Rule: Expand your horizons to expand your employability.

Epilogue:
Hitting That Home Run

♦♦♦

Gender was a non-issue for most corporations when we began writing *Hardball for Women*. In the year and a half since its publication, however, it has moved to the front burner. And so, rather than feeling quietly resentful, today women are openly questioning the powers-that-be about why there are so few females in the upper echelons of leadership. Hardball strategies may help you bridge this gap.

These may feel uncomfortable to you at first—putting them into practice may feel as if you're trying on someone else's jeans—because they sometimes require you to behave in ways that seem foreign and illogical. Once you achieve a powerful position, however, you will be able to change the game. And, as corporate structure flattens over the next decade, women's ways will be accepted and even rewarded. If women are to succeed in their careers they must band together and support each other. The future is ours if we seize it.

About the Authors

◆◆◆

Pat Heim, Ph.D. is a consultant, speaker, and trainer in leadership, communication, and gender differences. She has worked with CEOs, boards of directors, managers, and supervisors in many fields including manufacturing, health care, finance, engineering, and government. Founder of The Heim Group, she is based in West Los Angeles.

Susan K. Golant has authored numerous books on bio-psycho-social and women's issues and teaches nonfiction writing at UCLA's Writers' Program. She resides in West Los Angeles.

If you would like additional information on workshops
or resource materials you may write or call:

The Heim Group
P.O. Box 1745
Pacific Palisades, CA 90272
310-459-3178

She Said/He Said:
Gender Differences in the Workplace
A workshop designed for organizations looking to integrate
the diverse cultures of men and women.

Learning to Lead
A skills book for new managers.

Breakthrough Strategies for Women
Video recorded live from Pat Heim's Breakthrough Seminar.

She Said/He Said:
Gender Differences in the Workplace
Audio tape delineating the different worlds of men and women.